ULTIMATE NACHOS

ULTIMATE NACHOS

FROM NACHOS AND GUACAMOLE TO SALSAS AND COCKTAILS

FROM THE FOUNDERS OF NACHOS NY AND GUACTACULAR

LEE FRANK & RACHEL ANDERSON

PHOTOGRAPHS BY KAREN WISE

St. Martin's Griffin New York

www.stmartins.com

Design by Ralph Fowler / rlfdesign

ISBN 978-1-250-01654-6
(trade paperback)
ISBN 978-1-250-03973-6
(e-book)

First Edition: April 2013

10 9 8 7 6 5 4 3 2 1

To Ignacio Anaya: Thanks for your cheesy, crunchy contribution to the culinary world.

CONTENTS

DO YOU KNOW YOUR HISTORY?

Nachos originated in 1943 in Piedras Negras, Coahuila, Mexico. The brilliant Ignacio "Nacho" Anaya threw together a plate of cut tortillas, longhorn cheddar cheese, and jalapeño peppers when the wives of U.S. soldiers stationed nearby stopped by the Victory Club restaurant after the kitchen had closed. Ignacio put on his thinking cap and invented the dish, utilizing what ingredients were available to him.

Thus, nachos were born.

The word *nachos* first appeared in the Texan cookbook *A Taste of Texas* in 1949. "These nachos will help *El Capitan*—soon he will forget his troubles for nachos make one romantic."

In 1959, Carmen Rocha took nachos to California. They were loved so much by everyone who visited her Los Angeles restaurant El Cholo that she is often falsely credited as the creator.

It took another fifteen years for nachos to make it big-time, when concessions genius Frank Liberto reformulated nachos to chips with ooey-gooey cheese. He knew that if he served a snack this delicious at Arlington Stadium, he would be considered a visionary.

Despite Liberto's ingenuity, nachos still needed an extra boost to make it to the mainstream. That unexpected assistance came from national sportscaster Howard Cosell. During Monday Night Football broadcasts, Cosell loved how the word *nachos* rolled off his tongue so much that he proceeded to talk about them all night long.

Adding our own pages to the history of 'cho, Nachos NY began in the winter of 2009. Spawned from the obsession of Lee Frank, Lee along with Rachel Anderson began their nonstop quest to find the best nachos New York has to offer. Genetically predisposed to love cilantro, tolerate lactose, and handle jalapeño, Nachos NY will not stop until the United States of America is a Nachos Nation. Four Guactaculars (our annual guacamole-making competition), three Guac Rock boat cruises (the event where Guactacular winners re-create their guacamoles for fans to gorge on while listening to bands rock out), and six Nachos Crawls (an improvement on the bar crawl) later, Nachos NY continues to carve out a name for itself in nacho infamy.

Now, in 2013, nachos have been beaten down by 7-Eleven, AMC movie theaters, and Major League Baseball stadiums. This is the most important time to bring nachos back to their delicious beginnings.

Let us proceed.

WHAT ARE NACHOS?

Like the hot daughter of the local minister, nachos have a terrible reputation.

Blame the pink neon sign above the tiny cardboard boxes full of stale chips at your local convenience store. Blame the scary heat lamp at the movie theater. Blame the wiggly pump at the ball park that oozes glue-like yellow goo that should not legally be called cheese.

Whomever you blame, the truth hurts: The nacho, like Hollywood, isn't what it used to be. Good people of Nacho Nation, we cannot let this stand.

From our pedestal of pico pride, we offer, at this early stage in your nacho education, these official guidelines for what can (and cannot) be properly called nachos. Herewith, your Ten Commandments.

1. Nachos are not tortilla chips.

This is a common misnomer. This is as if someone picked up a hot dog bun and said, "What a gorgeous frank!"

2. Nachos are not that thing you eat at the movie theater.

That is nothing more than chips and dip. You don't call pita and hummus nachos, do you?

3. Know your setting.

We used to think that nachos were meant to be piled high and that individually plating nachos was heresy. However, over the past few years, we've realized that every nacho construction has its time. The mountain of nachos now lives in the realm of the outmoded high-five, while the individual nacho trades in the paper napkin for a linen napkin.

4. Nachos are not served on apple slices.

It's exciting that you want to be healthy. Good for you. Your mom will be proud. Have yourself some apple slices! Drizzle honey on top! Toss in some walnuts if you're feeling crazy. Just don't call them nachos, please. If someone looks at them and cannot guess they're nachos, they are not nachos.

5. Ingredients are key.

Nothing ruins nachos more than stale chips and poor ingredients. Do not use dry chicken breast left over from yesterday's rotisserie chicken. Do not use gooey, droopy refried beans from a bin. Nachos are a thing of beauty, not an excuse to clean your refrigerator. That's plain old gross.

6. Not all cheeses are created equal.

If your cheese glows in the dark, that is a nacho deal breaker. If your cheese comes in a jar that says "contains real cheese," run for cover.

7. Taco salad is not nachos.

There's a difference. A big, leafy green difference. Keep the lettuce out of this equation and there won't be any problems. We'll come back to this later on (page 70).

8. Nachos don't always require meat.

Chorizo is amazing, everyone obviously knows that. But nachos do not need meat to be incredible. So when a vegetarian says they can't eat nachos, slap them. Some of the world's best nachos are no more than chips, cheese, pico de gallo, guacamole, and jalapeños.

9. Get down and dirty.

Nachos are meant to be eaten with your hands. When the fork comes out, it's just not fun anymore. Lick your fingers, wipe them on your pant leg, and dig in. Stains are the new black.

10. Share with others.

This is the absolute most important edict to follow. Friends who 'cho together, bro together. Friends who 'cho together, grow together. Friends who 'cho together . . . well, you get the idea.

TORTILLA CHIPS

CHIPS YOU CAN USE

These chips are always up for using: white corn, yellow corn, and blue corn, sometimes red corn chips, when the corn is actually red.

CHIPS YOU CAN'T USE AND WHY

Round chips

This gripe has less to do with the chips than with what they represent. Circle chips are a reminder of movie theater nachos as well as being illogical. Unless you have an adorable-size tortilla press, you're not making tortillas in a circle that small. Tortilla chips are meant to be triangles so you can make the chips smaller without wasting any delicious corny goodness.

Scoops, strips, and colored chips

These are all silly gimmicks. One is an edible bowl, one is too narrow to hold nachos, and the last is a chip that has no place in nature.

Flavored chips

This is an obvious one, right? I would hope so. But I'm finding people tell me that they love making nachos with nacho cheese–flavored chips. You're spending the time to craft a delicious plate of nachos; you don't need to gunk it up with powdered cheese concoctions.

HOMEMADE TORTILLA CHIPS

1 ounce (2 tablespoons) vegetable or canola oil
1 corn tortilla
Salt
Cayenne pepper (optional)

This is the perfect place to start. You don't need to buy tortilla chips at the store to make nachos. If you buy corn tortillas, you will be impressed with the quality of the chips you produce. Consequently, you'll be disappointed with the chips aisle at the grocery store.

1. In a skillet over medium heat, heat the oil to 350°F. You'll know the oil is ready when you add a small piece of tortilla to the skillet and it floats and bubbles.
2. Cut round tortilla into triangle shapes of any size you want, then add the triangles to the oil.
3. When one side becomes golden brown, about 1 minute, flip them over and fry the opposite sides until golden brown.
4. Using a slotted spoon, remove the chips from the oil and transfer to paper towels to drain.
5. Toss the chips with salt and the cayenne, if using.

SALSA

Salsa is literally sauce. While traditional salsas predominantly feature tomatoes and peppers, we take that rule very liberally. When it comes to dipping chips and adding spice to nachos, the salsa can come from a variety of ingredients. We chose delicious ingredients such as clementines, mangoes, ginger, and pears to spice it up.

SIMPLE PICO DE GALLO

VEGAN • GLUTEN-FREE

MAKES 2 CUPS PICO DE GALLO

2 large tomatoes, seeded and diced
1 onion, diced
1 jalapeño pepper, minced
2 garlic cloves, diced
1 bunch fresh cilantro, coarsely chopped
Juice of 1 lime
Salt

When first learning to make salsas, it is easy to get carried away with ingredients; scale it back to this basic recipe for a delicious set of flavors. From this recipe you can build up to the most intricate of picos.

1. In a large bowl, combine the tomatoes, onion, jalapeño, and garlic.
2. Fold the chopped cilantro into the mixture.
3. Add the lime juice and season the pico de gallo with salt to taste.

FIRE-ROASTED TOMATILLO SALSA

VEGAN • GLUTEN-FREE

MAKES 2 CUPS SALSA

4 tomatillos, husks and stems removed
3 jalapeño peppers
Juice of ½ lime
1 bunch fresh cilantro, coarsely chopped
Salt

The tomatillo packs a sharper flavor than the tomato and works well with the light spice of jalapeños in this recipe.

1. Preheat the broiler to 500°F.
2. Place the tomatillos and jalapeños on a baking sheet and broil for 5 minutes.
3. Flip the tomatillos and jalapeños and broil for 5 minutes more.
4. Dice jalapeños and remove seeds.
5. In a food processor fitted with the metal blade, puree the tomatillos, jalapeños, lime juice, and cilantro until smooth.
6. Season the salsa with salt to taste.

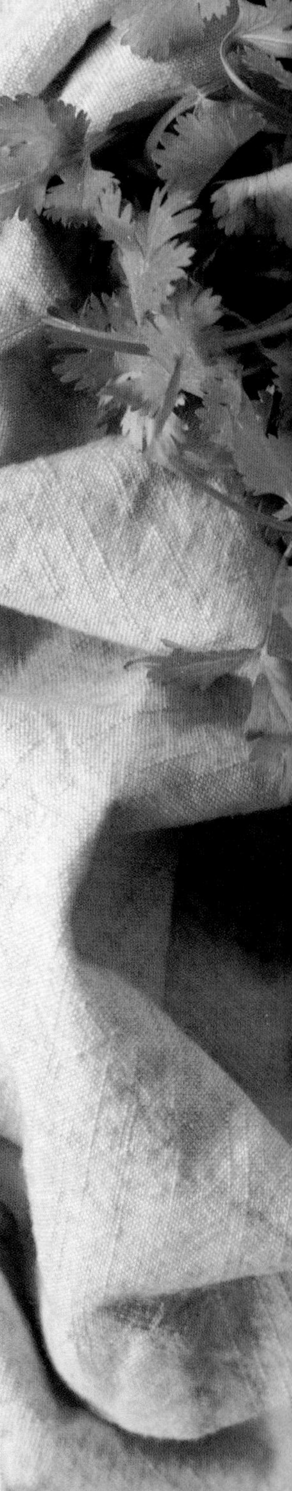

CLEMENTINE PICO DE GALLO

VEGAN • GLUTEN-FREE

MAKES 2 CUPS PICO DE GALLO

2 large tomatoes, seeded and diced
3 clementines, segmented, seeded, and diced
1 onion, diced
¼ jalapeño pepper, seeded and minced
1 lime, halved
Salt

For a sweet citrus to add to your repertoire, consider the adorable clementine. It's little and juicy and, in this recipe, makes salsa more refreshing than ever. Consider this salsa highly addictive.

1. In a large bowl, combine the tomatoes, clementines, onion, and jalapeño.
2. Squeeze the lime over the salsa and toss to combine.
3. Season the salsa with salt to taste.

PEAR-GINGER SALSA

VEGAN • GLUTEN-FREE

MAKES 2 CUPS SALSA

2 Bartlett pears, peeled, cored, and coarsely chopped
2 tablespoons fresh ginger, peeled and chopped
Juice of 2 limes
1 bunch fresh cilantro, coarsely chopped

Ginger is not often associated with salsa, but it plays a major role in this recipe, complementing the crisp taste of the pear.

1. In the bowl of a food processor fitted with the metal blade, puree the pears, ginger, lime juice, and cilantro.
2. Chill in a small bowl for 1 hour before serving.

PICKLED SERRANO AND MANGO PICO DE GALLO

VEGAN • GLUTEN-FREE

MAKES 2 CUPS PICO DE GALLO

2 Pickled Serrano Peppers (page 122)
1 mango, pitted, peeled, and diced
1 small onion, diced

This is the pico de gallo you bring to a barbecue along with some homemade tortilla chips to impress your friends. Once you've pickled the peppers, add the sweetness of mango to get taste buds applauding.

1. Dice the serrano peppers and remove the seeds depending on the desired spice level.
2. Add the mango and onion to the peppers and stir to combine.
3. Chill the pico for 1 hour to allow the flavors to meld.

ROASTED PINEAPPLE SALSA

VEGAN • GLUTEN-FREE

MAKES 3 CUPS SALSA

This Roasted Pineapple Salsa pairs perfectly with the Hawaiian Nachos (page 83). If you can, use dark rum to enhance the sweetness of the pineapple.

Olive oil or vegetable oil
1 pineapple, peeled, cored, and sliced into ½-inch rings
1 red bell pepper, seeded
1 jalapeño pepper, seeded
½ red onion, diced
½ cup coarsely chopped fresh cilantro
Juice of 2 limes
2 tablespoons dark rum
Salt and black pepper

1. Oil a grill grate on an outdoor grill or a stovetop grill with olive oil or vegetable oil. Place the pineapple rings, bell pepper, and jalapeño pepper on the grill.
2. Cook the pineapple until lightly browned on both sides, about 4 minutes per side. Continue to cook the bell pepper and jalapeño until blackened on all sides.
3. Dice the pineapple rings and set aside in a bowl. (If using the salsa for the Hawaiian Nachos [page 83], reserve 2 rings for garnish.)
4. Transfer the bell and jalapeño peppers to a paper or plastic bag and seal. As the steam from the pepper condenses, the skin becomes easier to peel off.
5. After about 5 minutes, and once the peppers are cool enough to handle, remove their skins, dice the peppers, and add to the diced pineapple.
6. Add the red onion, cilantro, lime juice, and rum and toss until well combined.
7. Season the salsa with salt and pepper to taste.

GUACAMOLE

In our minds, the avocado is the secret weapon of any nacho platter. It can go either way; a good guacamole elevates boring nachos, while gross guacamole ruins your day. In our long journey to this book, we have had the pleasure of hosting four Guactaculars. The Guactacular is our citywide search for the best guacamole recipe; starting off as a free Cinco de Mayo event, it got completely out of hand on its debut and we had to cut off future competitions at 300 attendees.

Every year, amateur hopefuls tweak on the traditional (Cumin at Ya Guacamole) or go a little crazy with their recipe (Raisin the Roof Guacamole) to wow the crowd and our esteemed judges. The winners go on to add their recipe to our summer boat cruise, Guac Rock, and, luckily for us, this book.

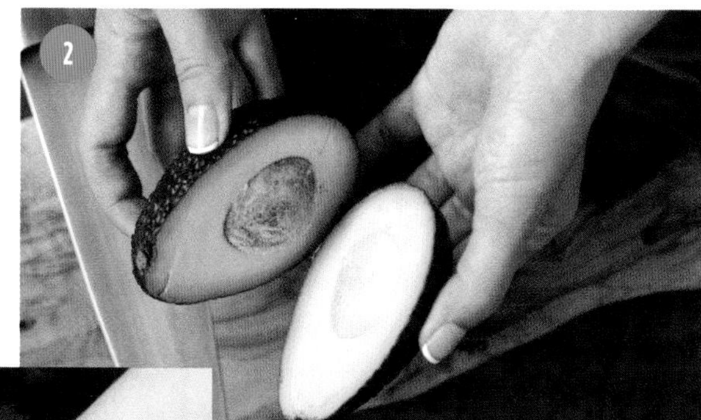

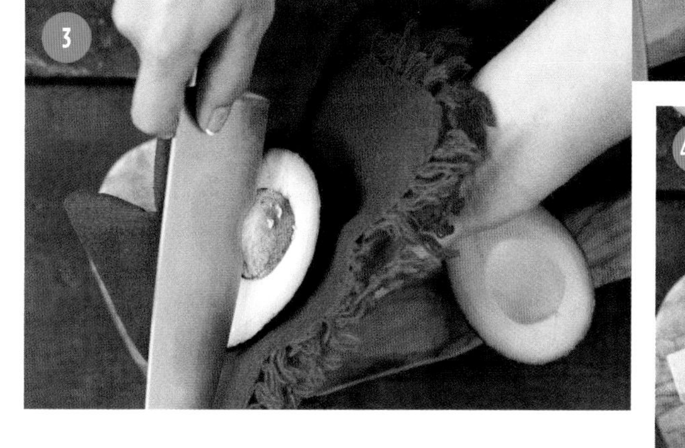

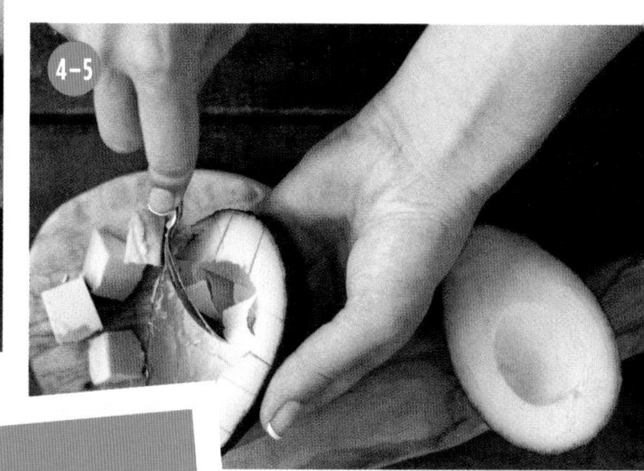

HOW TO PIT AN AVOCADO

1. Slice an avocado in half lengthwise.
2. Twist the two halves in opposite directions to separate.
3. Hold the half of the avocado containing the pit in a kitchen towel. Making guacamole shouldn't be dangerous! Using the bottom end of a chef's knife blade (closest to the handle), carefully knock it into the pit. Then twist the knife to remove the pit.
4. Slice the avocado in its skin with a paring knife.
5. Scoop out the flesh with a spoon.
6. Get to mashing!

SIMPLE GUACAMOLE

VEGAN • GLUTEN-FREE

MAKES 2 CUPS GUACAMOLE

2 avocados, halved lengthwise, pitted, and flesh scooped out
½ red onion, diced
½ tomato, seeded and diced
Juice of 1 lime
Salt

Purists will appreciate this recipe. Although we have heard that adding onions and tomatoes is a guacamole sacrilege, we love them and include them in our bare-bones guac.

1. In a medium bowl, mash the avocados with a fork.
2. Add the onion, tomato, and lime juice to the bowl.
3. Using a fork, fold the ingredients over each other to maintain the guacamole's chunkiness.
4. Season with salt to taste.

BACON-APPLE GUAC

GLUTEN-FREE

MAKES 3 CUPS GUACAMOLE

3 strips bacon
2 avocados, halved lengthwise, pitted, and flesh scooped out
1 Granny Smith apple, sliced
Salt and black pepper

Bacon will not be the hippest food forever, but while it is, we realize that bacon and avocado is a match made in heaven (try a BLAT—avocado BLT—sometime, it's great). The addition of the Granny Smith apple pushed this guac to the next level, a bona fide triple threat.

1. In a skillet over medium heat, fry the bacon until crispy. Flip and cook the opposite sides until crispy, 6 to 8 minutes per side. Transfer to paper towels to drain and cool.
2. Cut the bacon into small pieces.
3. In a bowl, mash the avocados with a fork.
4. Fold the bacon and apple into the mashed avocado.
5. Season with salt and pepper to taste.

TEQUILA MOCKINGBIRD GUACAMOLE

VEGAN • GLUTEN-FREE

MAKES 3 CUPS GUACAMOLE

3 avocados, halved lengthwise, pitted, and flesh scooped out
1 roasted red bell pepper, (see box), diced
1 jalapeño pepper, seeded and minced
2 garlic cloves, minced
Juice of 1 lime
2 tablespoons tequila
Salt and black pepper

This recipe was first served at Nachos NY's 2010 Guac Rock. A three-hour boat cruise along the East River, the event includes nine different guacamole recipes. In a pinch for a new flavor, Rachel just brought her guacamole bowl to the bar and asked them to free pour tequila into it. We've cleaned up this recipe to be served on dry land.

1. In a medium bowl, mash together the avocados, roasted red peppers, jalapeño peppers, and garlic with a fork.
2. Add the lime juice and tequila.
3. Season the guacamole with a generous amount of salt and pepper.

HOW TO ROAST A PEPPER

1. If you have a gas stove, place the bell pepper directly onto the grate. Using tongs, turn the pepper over the flame until black and charred on all sides.
2. If roasting the pepper in the oven, preheat the oven to 450°F. Line a baking sheet with aluminum foil, place pepper on the foil, then roast in the oven, turning the pepper every 15 minutes until blackened, 30 to 40 minutes.
3. Once the pepper is roasted, place it in a paper or plastic bag. As the steam from the pepper condenses, the skin becomes easier to peel off. Allow the pepper to cool for 5 minutes.
4. Carefully peel off the blackened skin and discard. This can be easily done with your fingers or using a sharp paring knife.
5. Cut off the top of the pepper and squeeze to clean out the seeds.

THE JOKER

VEGAN • GLUTEN-FREE

MAKES 3 CUPS GUACAMOLE

2 avocados, halved lengthwise, pitted, and flesh scooped out
2 garlic cloves, minced
Juice of 1 lime
Salt and black pepper
1 small beet, trimmed, peeled, and grated

Beets are sexy and this guac just proves it. The beet provides an earthy flavor to the guac while adding a visual twist. The vibrant purple color playing off the avocados' green hue pays tribute to Gotham's worst villain.

1. In a medium bowl, mash the avocados with the garlic and lime juice, using a fork.
2. Season with the salt and pepper.
3. Fold in the beet. Do not overmix.
4. Season again with salt and pepper to taste.

   NOTE: Again, we must stress: Do not overmix! The guacamole should have a green and purple color. Overmixing will turn the whole guacamole purple.

THE CLAP (CILANTRO-LIME-AVOCADO-POMEGRANATE) YOUR HANDS GUACAMOLE

Contributed by Karol Lu

VEGAN • GLUTEN-FREE

MAKES 3 CUPS GUACAMOLE

3 ripe avocados, halved lengthwise, pitted, and flesh scooped out
¼ cup finely chopped onion
1 jalapeño or serrano pepper, seeded, ribs removed, finely chopped
1 teaspoon ground cumin
1 teaspoon kosher salt
Juice of ½ lime
½ cup finely chopped fresh cilantro
½ cup pomegranate seeds

At our debut Guactacular, we found a way to cram about 360 people into a tiny bar space, and Karol Lu was crowned the winner with an incredibly simple guac made with four main ingredients that provided all of the flavor needed.

1. In a medium bowl, coarsely mash the avocados with a fork.
2. Add the onion, pepper, cumin, salt, and lime juice. Taste and adjust the seasoning as needed.
3. Fold in the cilantro and pomegranate seeds.

CUMIN AT YA GUACAMOLE

Contributed by Marcia Bunda

VEGAN • GLUTEN-FREE

MAKES 3 CUPS GUACAMOLE

3 avocados, halved lengthwise, pitted, and flesh scooped out
Juice of 4 limes
Roasted garlic from 1 large bulb of garlic (see box), mashed
1 cup diced onion
1 cup seeded and diced red bell pepper
3 to 5 jalapeño peppers, seeded and minced
1 tablespoon salt
1 teaspoon ground cumin

After we retooled the Guactacular to include a bigger space and a larger cast of competitors, Marcia Bunda took the People's Champion award with a guacamole featuring roasted garlic as the main attraction.

1. In a medium bowl, mash the avocados with a fork and immediately add the lime juice to prevent browning.
2. In a separate small bowl, mix together all of the remaining ingredients.
3. Gently combine the ingredients with the avocado. Taste and adjust the seasoning with more lime juice, jalapeño, salt, or cumin, as needed.
4. Cover the bowl tightly with plastic wrap, placing the wrap directly on the surface of the guacamole to preserve the color and prevent oxidation. Refrigerate and let the flavors meld for 2 to 3 hours before serving.

HOW TO ROAST GARLIC

Roasted garlic elevates the flavor of any guacamole, or you can simply mash it and spread it on toast. Garlic becomes so sweet once it has been roasted and caramelized that you'll be tempted to eat it straight from the oven.

1 garlic bulb
1 tablespoon olive oil
Salt and black pepper

1. Cut off the top one-third of a full bulb of garlic so that all the cloves are exposed.
2. Place the bulb on a sheet of aluminum foil, splash with olive oil, and sprinkle with salt.
3. Wrap the garlic up in the foil into a bulb shape, so that all the moisture escapes out of the twist at the top. Roast the garlic in a 400°F oven for 30 to 40 minutes.

RICOTTA AND RED ONION GUACAMOLE

Contributed by Peter Borenstein

VEGETARIAN • GLUTEN-FREE

MAKES 4 CUPS GUACAMOLE

3 avocados, halved lengthwise, pitted, and flesh scooped out
3 garlic cloves
Salt and black pepper
1 tomato, seeded and diced
½ red onion, diced
¼ cup chopped fresh cilantro
1 jalapeño pepper, seeded and minced
Juice of 2 limes
¾ cup ricotta cheese

In the 2010 Guactacular, Peter Borenstein wowed our panel of judges with the odd but surprisingly delicious addition of ricotta cheese to his guacamole.

1. In a medium bowl, mash the avocados with a fork and grate the garlic cloves with a cheese grater on top. Season the mixture with salt and pepper to taste.
2. Add the tomato, red onion, cilantro, and jalapeño. Add the lime juice. Season again with salt and pepper to taste.
3. Season the ricotta with salt only, then mix it in with the avocado until the mixture is creamy.

GINGER GUACAMOLE WITH VEGAN SRIRACHA MAYONNAISE

Contributed by Chris Willets

VEGAN • GLUTEN-FREE

MAKES 2 CUPS GUACAMOLE;
11/2 CUPS MAYONNAISE

24 perfect chips; if prepared fresh, use 4 corn tortillas, each cut into 6 triangles

Sriracha Mayonnaise

1 cup vegan mayonnaise
2 scallions, chopped
2 tablespoons sriracha sauce
Salt

Guacamole

2 avocados, halved lengthwise, pitted, and diced
1 tomato, seeded and diced
1 white onion, chopped
Juice of 1 lime
1 serrano pepper, seeded and minced
1 tablespoon fresh ginger, peeled and minced
Salt and black pepper

Garnish

5 radishes, sliced into ¼-inch slices
2 carrots, julienned
½ bunch fresh cilantro
½ cup coconut milk

Also placing in Guactacular 2010 was Chris Willets, whose guacamole comes assembled with a vegan mayo and a carrot and radish garnish.

1. In a bowl, mix together all of the ingredients for the Sriracha Mayonnaise. Refrigerate for 1 hour.
2. In a large bowl, coarsely mash the avocados with a fork. Fold in the tomato, white onion, lime juice, pepper, ginger, and salt and pepper, until you get a chunky yet creamy consistency.
3. To serve: Put a generous spoonful of the guac on each tortilla chip and top with 1 radish slice, a sprinkling of carrot, and a leaf or two of cilantro. Drizzle on some of the spicy mayonnaise and ½ teaspoon of coconut milk.

"AVICHE"—THE GUACAMOLE OF THE SEA

Contributed by Lindsay Liu, Ellie Ratcliff, and Lauren Cooper

GLUTEN-FREE

SERVES 4–6

Pickled Red Onion

1 cup water
1 red beet, peeled and quartered
¼ red onion, diced
1 tablespoon sugar
1 tablespoon white vinegar

Ceviche

½ pound fresh, white fish fillet, such as flounder
1 cup fresh lime juice (about 8 limes)
½ cup fresh lemon juice (about 2 lemons)
1 jalapeño pepper, seeded and minced
½ red onion, diced
½ Vidalia onion, diced
Pickled Red Onion (recipe above)
1 ear of corn, roasted, kernels removed (see box)
1 cucumber, peeled, seeded, and diced
1 mango, pitted, peeled, and diced
1 avocado, diced
3 avocados, halved lengthwise, pitted, flesh scooped out, and diced
Salt and black pepper

The judges loved this guacamole from Lindsay Liu, Ellie Ratcliff, and Lauren Cooper back in 2011. This is well put together, and turns the guacamole into a seafood cocktail.

To make the Pickled Red Onion

1. In a small saucepan, bring water to a boil. Add the beet to the water and boil for 5 minutes.
2. Add the red onion to the water along with the sugar and vinegar. Lower the heat and simmer for 10 minutes, until the onion is bright pink.
3. Remove the beet and drain the water. Set the onion aside.

To make the ceviche

1. Cut the fish into ½-inch pieces. In a shallow dish, cover the fish with the lime and lemon juice. Cover the dish with plastic wrap and refrigerate for about 20 minutes, or until the fish turns completely white, stirring as needed to keep all of the fish covered with the acid.
2. While the fish is "cooking" in the citrus juices, roast the corn (see box).
3. Once the fish is completely white, drain the majority of the lime and lemon juice, reserving enough to keep the fish wet, about ¼ cup.
4. Add the jalapeño, onions, roasted corn kernels, cucumber, mango, and diced avocado to the fish and mix together. Season the ceviche with salt and pepper to taste.
5. In a separate bowl, mash the avocados with a fork and add the reserved citrus juice, salt, and pepper to taste.
6. Serve the ceviche and guacamole layered on a tortilla chip and garnish with the Pickled Red Onion.

HOW TO ROAST CORN

1. Preheat the oven to 350°F.
2. Keep the husk on the corn and place the ear of corn directly on the oven rack.
3. Roast the corn for 30 minutes or until it is soft.
4. Peel down the husks and allow the corn to cool for 10 minutes, then remove the kernels with a sharp knife.

RAISIN THE ROOF GUACAMOLE

Contributed by Sofia Frank and Anthony DiSanti

VEGAN • GLUTEN-FREE

MAKES 2 CUPS GUACAMOLE

2 tablespoons diced white onion
½ jalapeño pepper, seeded and diced
1 small tomatillo, husked and diced
¼ cup finely chopped fresh cilantro
1 tablespoon diced roasted garlic (see How to Roast Garlic, page 25)
1 avocado, peeled, pitted, and diced
Juice of 1 lime
1 teaspoon unsweetened coconut flakes
2 teaspoons chopped raisins
1¼ teaspoons curry powder
Salt and black pepper

Sofia Frank and Anthony DiSanti took home the People's Champion award at 2011's Guactacular with this Thai-inspired guacamole. Who would have thought raisins could be such a guac-picker-upper?

1. In a medium bowl, combine the diced onion, jalapeño, tomatillo, cilantro, and garlic.
2. Add the avocado and lime juice to the diced ingredients. Using a fork, mix the ingredients together while also mashing the avocado.
3. Add the coconut, raisins, and curry powder and mix to combine.
4. Season with salt and pepper to taste.

ROCK OUT WITH YOUR GUAC OUT

Contributed by Alex Small

VEGETARIAN • GLUTEN-FREE

MAKES 3 CUPS GUACAMOLE;
1 CUP TOPPING

Guacamole

3 avocados, halved lengthwise, pitted, and flesh scooped out
Zest and juice of 1½ lemons
3 tablespoons chopped fresh oregano, or 2 tablespoons dried
1 jalapeño pepper, seeded and finely diced
¼ cup red onion, finely diced
Salt

Topping

1 cup sour cream
15 fresh chives, finely chopped
Zest of 1 lemon

Alex Small took home the People's Champion prize at Guactacular 2012. By swapping limes for lemons and adding oregano and chives, you can create a fan favorite at your next party.

To make the guacamole

1. In a medium bowl, mash the avocados with a fork.
2. Gently fold in the lemon zest, lemon juice, oregano, jalapeño, and onion, and season with salt to taste until the ingredients are mixed; be careful not to overstir.

To make the topping

1. In a separate small bowl, mix together the sour cream, chives, and lemon zest to make the topping.
2. Spread the topping over the guacamole and serve.

QUESO AND CHEESE SAUCE

Béchamel sauce, also known as white sauce, is one of the mother sauces of French cuisine. It is made by whisking hot milk into a flour and butter mixture, known as a roux, and seasoned with a little nutmeg.

Now, how does this relate to nachos, you may ask? Well, simply add your favorite cheese and you have an easy and delicious cheese sauce.

Some tips for making a tasty cheese sauce: Make sure to shred or grate the cheese prior to putting it in the sauce, keep the heat low, and stir until all the cheese has melted and been incorporated evenly. You should also make sure to select a cheese that melts well. Cheeses like cheddar, blue cheese, Monterey Jack, and Gouda will produce a rich, smooth cheese sauce. However, several Mexican cheeses like queso blanco, queso fresco, and cotija, and other cheeses like Parmigiano-Reggiano and ricotta will not melt well; and cheeses like provolone and mozzarella are too stringy to use in a smooth cheese sauce.

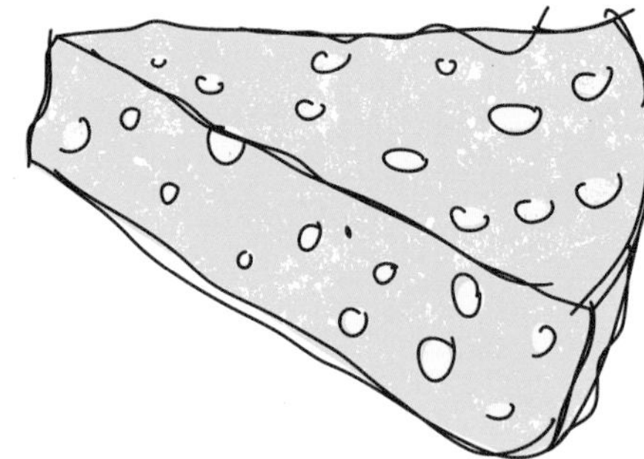

BÉCHAMEL CHEESE SAUCE

VEGETARIAN

MAKES 2 CUPS SAUCE

2 tablespoons unsalted butter
2 tablespoons all-purpose flour
2 cups whole milk
8 ounces melting cheese of your choice, shredded (about 2 cups)
Salt and black pepper

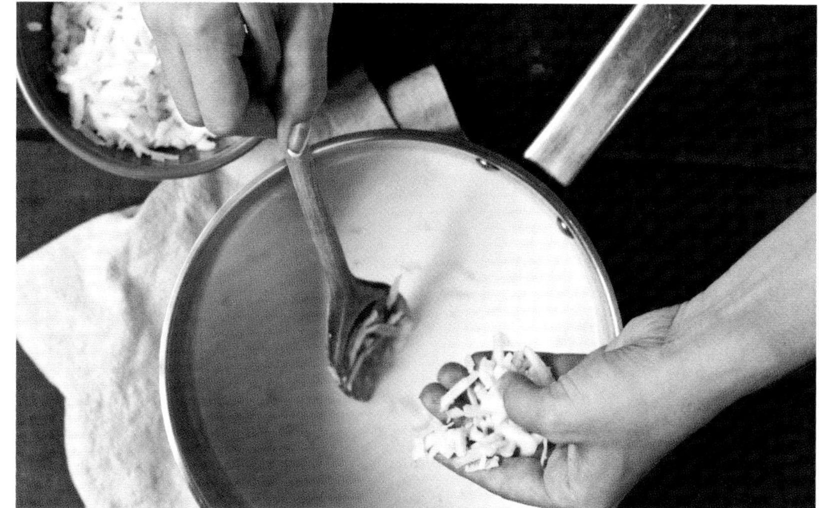

Often known as a Mornay or white sauce, this is definitely a step up from that neon-orange cheese sauce you get at the movie theater. Based on the mother of all sauces, béchamel sauce, this recipe is the basis of all the cheese sauce recipes that will be used throughout the book.

1. In a medium saucepan, melt the butter over medium-low heat.
2. Add the flour and stir until a smooth paste forms, 5 to 6 minutes.
3. Meanwhile, in a separate pan, heat the milk until it is just about to boil. Be careful not to burn the milk. Burnt milk is cringe-worthy.
4. Gradually add the hot milk to the butter mixture, and whisk continuously until smooth. Bring the sauce to a boil.
5. Cook for 10 minutes, stirring constantly, then remove from the heat, immediately add the shredded cheese, and stir together until evenly incorporated.
6. Season the cheese sauce with salt and pepper to taste.

QUESO BLANCO

Contributed by Ivy Stark, Executive Chef at Dos Caminos

VEGETARIAN

MAKES 4 CUPS QUESO

3 tablespoons unsalted butter
1 medium onion, diced
3 serrano peppers, finely diced
3 tablespoons all-purpose flour
2 cups half-and-half, warmed
½ teaspoon ground cumin
1 teaspoon dried Mexican oregano
4 poblano peppers, diced
1½ cups chihuahua cheese (about 6 ounces), shredded
6 ounces muenster cheese, shredded
1 tablespoon fresh lime juice
1 tablespoon fresh cilantro, shredded
½ ear roasted corn, kernels removed (see How to Roast Corn, page 31)
One 4-ounce jar pickled jalapeño peppers, diced

In working with Dos Caminos and writing the book *Dos Caminos' Mexican Street Food,* Chef Ivy Stark had the opportunity to work with a variety of delicious flavors. Here she shares her recipe for a deliciously spicy queso with us. The Mexican oregano is used for its citrus flavor, which pairs very well with the peppers in this recipe.

1. In a saucepan over medium heat, melt the butter. Add the diced onion and serranos and sauté until the onion is soft and translucent.
2. Add the flour and stir, scraping the bottom of the pan to prevent sticking. Cook for several minutes to remove the raw flour taste from the roux.
3. Whisk in the heated half-and-half and cook until the sauce has thickened; it will coat the back of a spoon.
4. Add the cumin, Mexican oregano, and poblano peppers and stir to combine.
5. Add the cheeses and stir over medium heat until they have fully melted.
6. Stir in the lime juice.
7. Sprinkle with the cilantro, corn kernels, and pickled jalapeños and serve with warm corn tortillas or chips.

VEGAN WHITE BEAN QUESO

Contributed by The Brooklyn Salsa Company

VEGAN • GLUTEN-FREE

MAKES 6 CUPS QUESO

1½ cups dried white beans
¼ cup tahini
1 tablespoon olive oil
½ cup water, preferably purified
½ cup fresh cilantro, coarsely chopped
1 teaspoon sea salt
6 garlic cloves
Juice of 2 limes
One 16-ounce jar prepared salsa

Our good friends at The Brooklyn Salsa Company are known for specializing in salsa that can be found all around the globe. They had a hunch that they could make a queso that is both delicious and vegan. They were right.

1. Fill a large bowl with warm water and soak the beans overnight.
2. The following day, discard the water and rinse the beans.
3. Boil the beans in fresh water for about 1 hour until they are extremely soft.
4. Drain and discard the water and rinse the beans.
5. Combine all of the ingredients in a food processor or blender and puree until smooth.
6. Warm the queso on the stovetop before serving as a dip for chips and veggies, or straight up on tortilla chips. This is also delicious cold.

NACHOS IN SMALL BITES

When nachos were born, they were a single chip with Longhorn cheddar and jalapeños. While we often opt for massive platters of nachos, in this section we pay homage to the historical appetizer-style nachos. After we teach you how to make Nachos Especiales (as Ignacio Anaya would have wanted), we embellish the appetizer idea by turning the recipes into old-school favorites like Personal Pepperoni Pizza Nachos and innovative starters like Nacho Dumplings and Fried Calamari Nachos.

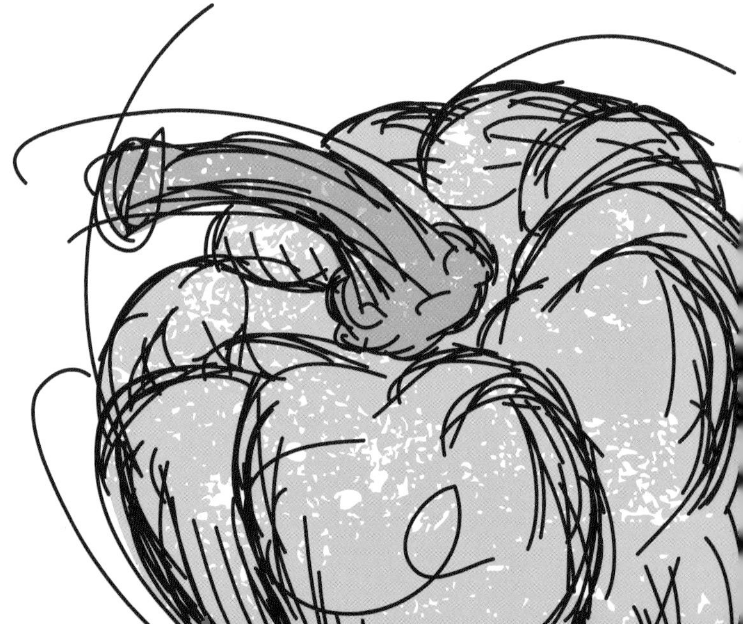

NACHOS ESPECIALES—THE ORIGINAL NACHOS

VEGETARIAN • GLUTEN-FREE

SERVES 3

18 perfect chips; if prepared fresh, use 3 corn tortillas, each cut into 6 triangles
4 ounces Longhorn cheddar cheese, shredded (about 1 cup)
18 jarred pickled jalapeño slices

As Ignacio himself prepared decades before, the original nachos are simple, quick, and to the point—chips, cheese, and a little kick of jalapeño in every bite. Serve them with the Simple Pico de Gallo (page 7) and Simple Guacamole (page 18) for a classic treat!

1. Preheat the broiler to 500°F.
2. Evenly spread out the chips on a baking sheet.
3. On each chip, equally distribute the shredded cheddar cheese, about 1 tablespoon per chip.
4. Place the chips under the broiler for 5 minutes until the cheese has melted.
5. Top each chip with a pickled jalapeño slice.

PERSONAL PEPPERONI PIZZA NACHOS

GLUTEN-FREE

SERVES 4

32 perfect chips; if prepared fresh, use 4 corn tortillas each cut into 8 triangles
3 Thai or finger peppers, diced
One 8-ounce can tomato paste
6 ounces mozzarella cheese, shredded (about 1½ cups)
16 pepperoni slices
16 small fresh basil leaves

This is the ultimate after-school snack that will transform any mom into the coolest mom in the neighborhood. Thai peppers (also known as finger peppers) are small, multicolored peppers that we used in this recipe to pack a punch.

1. Combine the finger peppers with the tomato paste. Allow the paste to sit for 30 minutes.
2. Preheat the broiler to 500°F.
3. On a parchment paper–lined baking sheet, arrange 8 chips into the shape of a personal pan pizza. Repeat to make a total of four pan pizzas.
4. Using a spoon, spread the tomato paste sauce on each chip. Sprinkle the shredded cheese evenly on the chips. Top each chip with a pepperoni slice.
5. Broil the nachos for 8 minutes, or until the cheese has melted.
6. Garnish each chip with a basil leaf.

CROQUE MONSIEUR NACHOS

GLUTEN-FREE

SERVES 3

18 perfect chips; if prepared fresh, use 3 corn tortillas, each cut into 6 triangles
9 slices thin-sliced ham
9 slices thin-sliced Emmental cheese
3 tablespoons Dijon mustard

The Croque Monsieur is essentially a ham and cheese sandwich, but uses Emmental cheese and Dijon mustard, because the French are fancy like that. If you want to make the lady version of these nachos, the Croque Madame, add a fried egg on top of the chips once they come out of the oven. And don't be afraid to break out a knife and fork for these nachos!

1. Preheat the broiler to 500°F.
2. Evenly spread out the chips on a baking sheet.
3. Cut the ham and Emmental slices in half to yield 18 slices each.
4. Spread about ½ teaspoon of the Dijon mustard on each chip. Top each chip with the ham and then drape the Emmental cheese over the meat.
5. Place the chips under the broiler for 5 minutes.

REUBEN NACHOS

GLUTEN-FREE

SERVES 3

18 perfect chips; if prepared fresh, use 3 corn tortillas, each cut into 6 triangles
9 slices thin-sliced corned beef
9 slices thin-sliced Swiss cheese
½ cup sauerkraut
Thousand Island Crema (page 120)

The Reuben is a classic sandwich that everybody loves. Top with our Thousand Island Crema (page 120) and enjoy! For a variation on the Reuben, why not make some Rachel Nachos? Swap the corned beef and sauerkraut for pastrami and coleslaw for another tasty spin on this sandwich-inspired treat!

1. Preheat the broiler to 500°F.
2. Evenly spread out the chips on a baking sheet.
3. Cut the corned beef and Swiss cheese slices in half to yield 18 slices.
4. Top each chip with a slice of corned beef and then drape a slice of Swiss cheese over the meat.
5. Place the chips under the broiler for 5 minutes.
6. Remove from the broiler and top the chips with the sauerkraut, then drizzle the crema evenly over the chips.

FRIED CALAMARI NACHOS

SERVES 4

½ pound calamari, tubes only
1 cup panko bread crumbs
1 tablespoon Italian seasoning
1 teaspoon salt
1 teaspoon ground black pepper
Vegetable oil, for frying
7 ounces corn tortilla chips, approximately half of a store-bought bag, or, if prepared fresh, use 15 corn tortillas, each cut into 6 triangles
8 ounces mozzarella cheese, shredded (about 2 cups)
¾ cup prepared marinara sauce
1 lemon, halved

It's so easy to screw up seafood nachos. For instance, cheddar cheese and lobster should stay far, far away from each other. However, in this recipe, calamari pairs nicely with mozzarella. To prevent the chips from getting soggy and the marinara from drying out, add the marinara sauce after the chips, cheese, and fried calamari have baked in the oven.

1. Preheat the oven to 350°F.
2. Thinly slice the calamari into rings about ½ inch thick.
3. Mix the panko, Italian seasoning, salt, and pepper in a large bowl. Toss the calamari in the panko mixture to coat.
4. Fry the calamari in the vegetable oil in a deep fryer or in a heavy-bottomed pot heated to 350°F, until golden brown, about 1 minute.
5. Transfer the fried calamari to a paper towel–lined plate.
6. Layer the tortilla chips in a 9 x 13-inch roasting pan. Evenly distribute the fried calamari over the chips. Cover the chips with the shredded cheese.
7. Bake the nachos for 10 to 15 minutes until the cheese has melted.
8. While the nachos are in the oven, heat the marinara sauce in a small saucepan over medium heat. Evenly drizzle the warmed marinara sauce over the nachos and squeeze the juice from the lemon halves over the nachos.

TOSTADAS DE JAIBA EN SALPICON

Contributed by Hugo Ortega, Executive Chef at Hugo's

GLUTEN-FREE

SERVES 4

This "can't-miss" appetizer from the author of *Hugo Ortega's Street Food of Mexico* and executive chef of Hugo's in Houston, Texas, will be the hit of your next dinner party. Simple, delicious, and *muy auténtico.*

Tostada

2 tablespoons olive oil
1 garlic clove, minced
1 serrano pepper, diced
2 bay leaves
1 small onion, finely chopped
¼ teaspoon dried oregano
¼ teaspoon dried thyme
2 small red potatoes
1 pound jumbo lump crabmeat
7 ounces corn tortilla chips, approximately half of a store-bought bag, or, if prepared fresh, use 15 corn tortillas, each cut into 6 triangles
3 unpeeled radishes, cut into very fine matchsticks

Dressing

1 cup olive oil
¼ cup white vinegar
¼ cup fresh lime juice
¼ cup finely chopped fresh tomatoes
Salt and black pepper

1. Heat the olive oil in a sauté pan.
2. Add the garlic, serrano pepper, bay leaves, dried herbs, and onion. Sauté for 5 minutes, then cool to room temperature. Remove and discard the bay leaves.
3. Boil the potatoes in salted water for 10 to 15 minutes until tender. Then let them cool to room temperature.
4. When cool enough to handle, peel the potatoes and dice finely.
5. Combine the crabmeat, potatoes, and herb mixture. Set aside.
6. Whisk together all of the ingredients for the dressing.
7. Add approximately half of the dressing mixture to the crabmeat mixture, toss to combine, and refrigerate for at least one hour.
8. Arrange the chips on a serving platter and spoon the crabmeat mixture on top. Drizzle with the remaining dressing and garnish with the radishes.

NACHO DUMPLINGS WITH GINGER-SESAME SALSA AND AVOCADO-HORSERADISH CREMA

Contributed by Lindsay Liu of Dumpering.com

SERVES 4 FOR DINNER OR 8 FOR SNACK-SIZE PORTIONS

Ginger-Sesame Salsa

1 beefsteak tomato, diced
1 vine-ripened tomato, diced
½ red onion, diced
½ Vidalia onion, diced
1 teaspoon fresh minced garlic
2 scallions, chopped
1 teaspoon toasted white sesame seeds
½ teaspoon salt
½ teaspoon ancho chili powder
1 teaspoon sesame oil
Juice of ¼ lime

Dumplings

1 beefsteak tomato, diced
1 cup shredded red lettuce
Juice of ½ lime
1 teaspoon salt
Canola oil
1 yellow onion, diced
1 pound ground beef
1 cup shredded cheddar cheese
Black pepper
1 pack dumpling skins (50/pack)
Ginger-Sesame Salsa (recipe above)
Avocado-Horseradish Crema (page 120)

Lindsay Liu is a big fan of dumplings. She proves it all the time on her Dumpling blog, Dumpering.com. In this recipe she lends us a hand with a nacho recipe inside a delicious dumpling.

To make the salsa

1. Mix together all of the ingredients and let the salsa sit in the refrigerator for at least 2 hours before serving.

To make the dumplings

1. In a bowl, mix half of the tomato and all of the lettuce with the lime juice and salt. Set aside.
2. Heat 1 tablespoon of oil in a skillet on medium heat.
3. Add the onion and the remaining half of the tomato to the skillet and cook until soft. Add the ground beef and cook until medium rare, 5 to 7 minutes.
4. Remove the skillet from the heat and add the beef mixture to the bowl with the tomato and lettuce, then mix in the cheese and season with pepper to taste.
5. Add a tablespoon of the beef mixture to the center of the dumpling skin.
6. Fold the skin once along the top and leave the sides open.
7. In a skillet over medium heat, add enough oil to cover the entire bottom of the skillet.
8. Panfry the dumplings in the skillet until golden and crispy on the bottom. Flip once and panfry on the opposite sides.
9. Serve hot with the Ginger-Sesame Salsa and Avocado-Horseradish Crema.

NACHOS FOR BREAKFAST

Ever have a glass of orange juice or a nice latte with your nachos? Probably not. But with the following recipes, when you wake up in the morning after dreaming about nachos, you can fix yourself a plate to start off your day. We have always wanted to eat nachos all day long, and with the addition of eggs to our nachos, we have figured out how to squeeze another serving into our day.

SUNNY-SIDE NACHOS

GLUTEN-FREE

SERVES 4

1 pound ground breakfast sausage (vegetarians can substitute Gimme Lean)
Cayenne pepper
7 ounces corn tortilla chips, approximately half of a store-bought bag, or, if prepared fresh, use 15 corn tortillas, each cut into 6 triangles
1 white onion, diced
1 medium tomato, seeded and diced
8 ounces cheddar cheese, shredded (about 2 cups, divided)
4 large eggs

Breakfast is the most important meal of the day and nachos are the most important dish ever. So this is a match made in heaven.

1. Preheat the oven to 350°F.
2. In a skillet, crumble and brown the breakfast sausage as per the package directions. Sprinkle in some cayenne for an additional kick.
3. Layer the tortilla chips in a 9 x 13-inch roasting pan. Evenly distribute the sausage, onion, and tomato over the chips. Cover the chips with 1½ cups shredded cheese.
4. Bake the nachos for 10 to 15 minutes until the cheese has melted.
5. While the nachos are baking, fry 4 eggs sunny side up, leaving the yolks runny.
6. When the nachos are done, place the eggs directly on top of the nachos. Sprinkle the remaining ½ cup shredded cheese over the eggs and season generously with salt and pepper.
7. Serve the nachos with a side of home fries and a hot cup of coffee.

NACHOS WITH ASPARAGUS AND HOLLANDAISE SAUCE

Contributed by Cathy Erway, Founder of NotEatingOutInNY.com

GLUTEN-FREE

SERVES 6 TO 8

This recipe is a take on a classic French vegetable side, placed on a bed of nachos! You can add small cubes of ham, or leave them out for a vegetarian (but still very rich) version.

Nachos

1 bunch fresh asparagus
7 ounces corn tortilla chips, approximately half of a store-bought bag, or, if prepared fresh, use 15 corn tortillas, each cut into 6 triangles
½ cup cubed ham (¼-inch cubes, optional)
6 ounces cheddar cheese, shredded (about 1½ cups)
Hollandaise Sauce (recipe below)
2 to 3 tablespoons chopped fresh chives

Hollandaise Sauce

1 egg yolk, at room temperature
8 tablespoons (1 stick) unsalted butter, melted
2 teaspoons fresh lemon juice
Pinch of salt and black pepper

To prepare the nachos

1. Trim the tough ends from each asparagus stalk by snapping it where it naturally breaks, near the stem, then cut on the diagonal into ½-inch pieces.
2. Preheat the oven to 375°F.
3. Spread the chips out in a deep baking dish or casserole. Evenly distribute the asparagus and ham, if using, on top. Cover the chips with the shredded cheese.
4. Bake the nachos until the cheese is fully melted, about 10 minutes.

To make the Hollandaise Sauce

1. Whisk the egg yolk. Make sure the butter is fully melted, then slowly drizzle the butter, a little bit at a time, into the yolk while whisking constantly. Drizzle in the lemon juice, and add salt and pepper to taste.
2. Remove the nachos from the oven and drizzle the sauce evenly across the top.
3. Sprinkle with the chives and serve immediately.

BREAKFAST NACHOS SKILLET

VEGETARIAN • GLUTEN-FREE

SERVES 4

2 tablespoons olive oil, divided
1 onion, diced
2 leeks, white parts only, chopped
Salt and black pepper
One 6-ounce bag baby spinach
Juice of 1 lemon
7 ounces corn tortilla chips, approximately half of a store-bought bag, or, if prepared fresh, use 15 corn tortillas, each cut into 6 triangles
8 ounces fresh mozzarella cheese, thinly sliced
4 large eggs, preferably organic if you prefer runny eggs
10 cherry tomatoes, halved

Break out the cast-iron skillet—it's time for a nachos bake.

1. Preheat the oven to 350°F.
2. Heat a sauté pan over medium heat until hot. Add 1 tablespoon of the olive oil to the pan and swirl to coat.
3. After a minute add the onion and leeks to the pan and season with the salt. Cook the vegetables until translucent and tender.
4. Add the spinach and continue to cook, turning the spinach over, until wilted and coated in oil. Add the lemon juice and continue to cook.
5. Meanwhile, evenly arrange the tortilla chips in a cast-iron skillet. (An oven-safe 10-inch pan will work as well.) Cover the chips with half of the cooked spinach-leek mixture. Evenly distribute the fresh mozzarella slices over the vegetables. Spread the remaining vegetables over the cheese.
6. Make four wells an equal distance apart in the vegetable mixture. Crack an egg into each well.
7. In a small bowl, toss the halved cherry tomatoes in the remaining 1 tablespoon olive oil, and season with salt and pepper. Evenly distribute the tomatoes around the edge of the skillet to garnish.
8. Bake the nachos skillet in the oven for 15 minutes, or until the egg whites have firmed up. Bake for longer if you do not like runny eggs.

CHILAQUILES VERDES WITH PEPITAS AND PICKLED RED ONION AND JALAPEÑO

Contributed by J. Kenji López-Alt, Chief Creative Officer at Serious Eats

SERVES 4 TO 6

Chilaquiles Verdes Sauce

1 small onion, roughly chopped
2 garlic cloves, minced
1 jalapeño or serrano pepper, seeded and halved
1 large poblano pepper, stemmed and halved
1 pound tomatillos (12 to 16 medium), stemmed, husked, and halved
1 tablespoon vegetable oil
Kosher salt
1 cup loosely packed cilantro leaves

Pickled Red Onion and Jalapeño

½ cup sugar
2 teaspoons salt
½ cup water
½ cup distilled white vinegar
1 small medium red onion, thinly sliced (about 1 cup)
1 jalapeño pepper, cut into ⅛-inch slices

(continued)

When you write a column entitled "The Food Lab," you better be scientifically proven to produce delicious food. J. Kenji López-Alt, Chief Creative Officer at Serious Eats, taste tested this recipe until it was perfect.

To make the Chilaquiles Verdes Sauce

1. Preheat the broiler to 500°F.
2. Mix the onion, garlic, peppers, and tomatillos in a large bowl. Drizzle with oil, season with kosher salt, and toss to coat evenly with the oil.
3. Line a heavy-duty rimmed baking sheet with aluminum foil and spread out the Chilaquiles Verde Sauce ingredients.
4. Broil, turning occasionally, until the ingredients are completely softened and well-charred on a few surfaces, about 15 minutes.
5. Remove from the broiler and transfer to a blender along with any collected juices. Add the cilantro and blend until smooth, starting slowly and gradually increasing the speed to prevent explosion. Season to taste with salt and set aside.

To make the Pickled Red Onions and Jalapeño

1. Combine the sugar, salt, water, and vinegar in a small saucepan. Bring to a boil over high heat, whisking frequently until the sugar and salt are dissolved.
2. Remove the saucepan from the heat and add the onion and jalapeño, pressing them down into the liquid. Cover tightly and let stand for 2 minutes, then stir to redistribute. Let stand 10 minutes more. Set the saucepan aside.

(continued)

Chilaquiles

- Chilaquiles Verdes Sauce (page 58)
- Pickled Red Onion and Jalapeño (page 58)
- 1 cup low-sodium chicken broth
- 7 ounces corn tortilla chips, approximately half of a store-bought bag, or, if prepared fresh, use 15 corn tortillas, each cut into 6 triangles
- ¼ cup grated cotija cheese
- ⅓ cup Mexican crema or Basic Crema (page 119)
- ¼ cup toasted pepitas (pumpkin seeds)

To assemble the chilaquiles

1. Preheat the oven to 350°F and don't forget to readjust your oven rack so it's in the middle position.
2. Transfer the verde sauce and chicken broth to a large saucepan and bring to a simmer.
3. Remove from the heat, add the chips, and carefully fold them in until totally coated with the sauce.
4. Transfer the chips to a large ovenproof casserole dish. Sprinkle the chips with cotija cheese.
5. Bake until the chilaquiles are slightly dried around the edges and the cheese is very lightly browned, about 10 minutes.
6. Remove from the oven, drizzle with crema, sprinkle with pepitas, and scatter a handful of the pickled red onion and jalapeño over the top. (Any extra onions can be stored in a sealed container in the fridge for up to 2 weeks.) Serve immediately.

NACHO CHEESE SNACKS

When I imagine nacho cheese-flavored snacks, my mind races to thoughts of bad '90s commercials with a surfboard riding a tidal wave of flavor on every bite. It is as though three guys in white lab coats with neon-orange stains from dehydrated cheddar powder are high-fiving as they discover the nacho-cheesiest snack in the history of food.

Doritos is certainly a source of the Nacho Cheese onslaught—their "tortilla-style" chip debuted way back in 1972 and has been so good for Doritos that their founder, Arch West, was buried with the cheesy snack.

In a move that has many saying "duh," Taco Bell released the Doritos Locos Taco with a Nacho Cheese shell, which has been wildly successful. Now the mad scientists at Taco Bell and Doritos are hard at work perfecting the Cool Ranch iteration.

Since starting Nachos NY four years ago, we've reviewed and reviled nacho-flavored crackers, peanuts, beef jerky, sunflower seeds, and a lot more strange orange-colored foods. They are terrible. Terrible and rampant.

We're not trying to disparage inventors from finding the shortcut to delicious (we have eaten our share of nacho cheese snacks), but we are saying that you shouldn't confuse these foods with nachos.

—Lee

SAGE BROWN BUTTER ARTICHOKE NACHOS

VEGETARIAN • GLUTEN-FREE

SERVES 4

- 6 tablespoons (¾ stick) unsalted butter
- 8 sage leaves
- One 14-ounce can artichoke hearts, drained, quartered
- 7 ounces corn tortilla chips, approximately half of a store-bought bag, or, if prepared fresh, use 15 corn tortillas, each cut into 6 triangles
- 8 ounces mozzarella cheese, shredded (approximately 2 cups)
- Black pepper

Brown butter is ridiculously easy to make and elevates the flavor of any dish, sweet or savory. (Next time you are making a basic vanilla cake, brown the butter first to give it a deep, nutty flavor.) For this recipe, when the sage leaves have been cooking in the brown butter, they become crispy. It's hard not to pop a few in your mouth before serving.

1. Preheat the oven to 350°F.
2. To prepare the sage brown butter: Slice the butter into tablespoon-size pieces, place in a small saucepan, and melt over medium heat.
3. Once the butter has melted, add the sage leaves. Continue to cook until light brown bits form at the bottom of the pan; be very careful not to burn the butter, just brown it. The sage leaves will be crunchy and the butter should have a nutty aroma.
4. Toss the artichoke quarters in the sage brown butter to coat.
5. Layer the tortilla chips in a 9 x 13-inch roasting pan. Evenly distribute the sage brown butter and artichoke mixture, then cover the chips with the shredded cheese.
6. Bake the nachos for 10 to 15 minutes until the cheese has melted.
7. Season with black pepper to taste and then serve.

THE MAIN EVENT

Sometimes, nachos are the main event. Two occasions when nachos are the most important thing: the Super Bowl and your wedding. For these occasions, you have to bring out the big guns. In this section, we introduce your kitchen to chorizo, jerk chicken, lamb chili, and more, and get you ready for a glorious food coma.

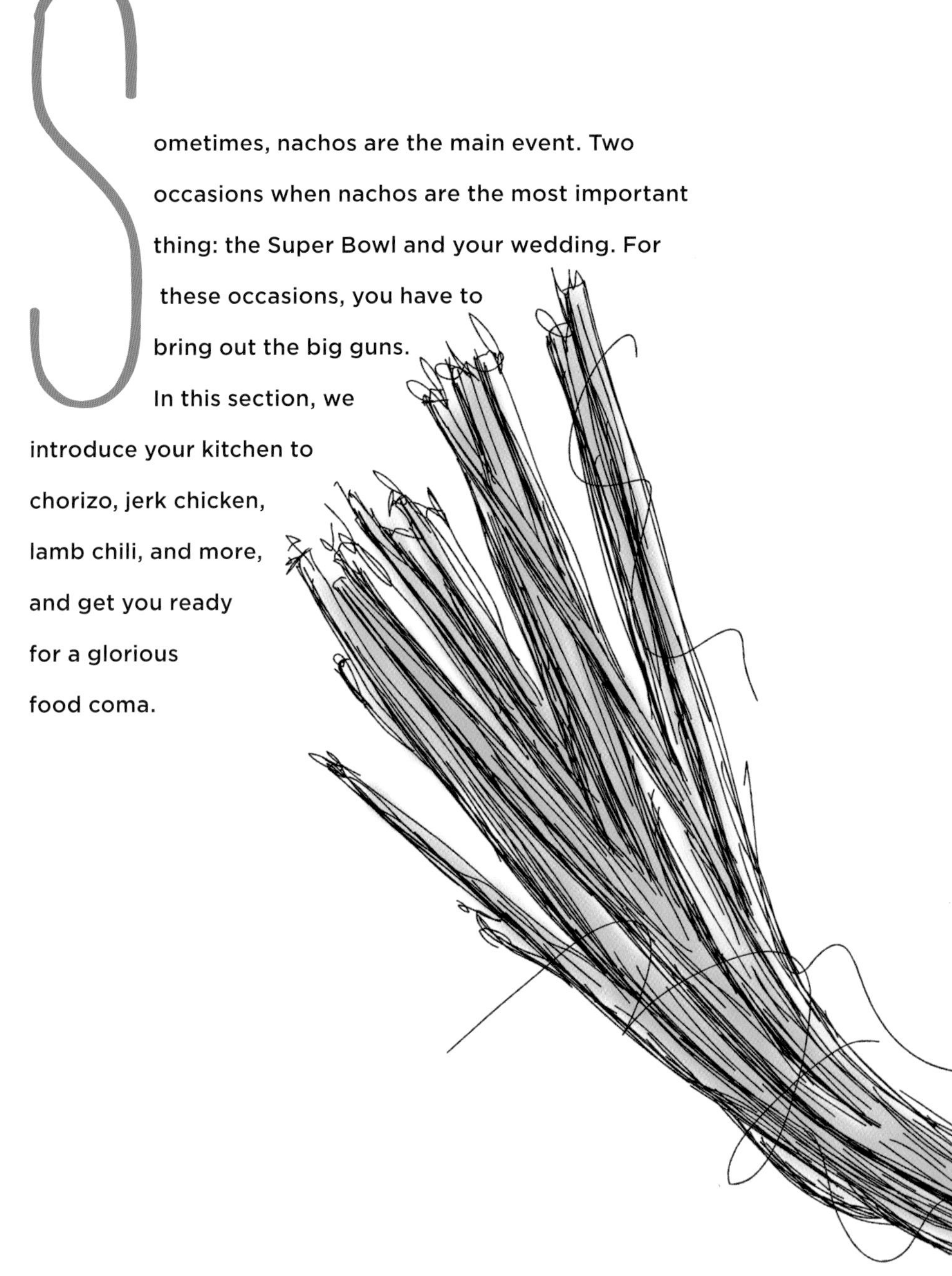

PHILLY CHEESESTEAK NACHOS

SERVES 4

1 tablespoon olive oil
½ red onion, diced
½ red or green bell pepper, seeded and diced
½ pound thinly sliced beef, chopped
7 ounces corn tortilla chips, approximately half of a store-bought bag, or, if prepared fresh, use 15 corn tortillas, each cut into 6 triangles
1 tomato, seeded and diced
1 cup Béchamel Cheese Sauce (page 35), made with cheddar, warmed

When it comes to growing up in Philly, at an early age you have to decide two things: with or without onions, and if you want it with Cheez Whiz. Let the record show: with onions and whiz for me. —*Lee*

1. In a small pan over medium heat add the olive oil. Add the onion and pepper and sauté until the onion is translucent, about 5 minutes.
2. Add the beef and cook until brown.
3. Layer the chips in a 9 x 13-inch roasting pan and evenly distribute the beef, onion, pepper, and diced tomato.
4. Cover the chips with the warm cheese sauce.

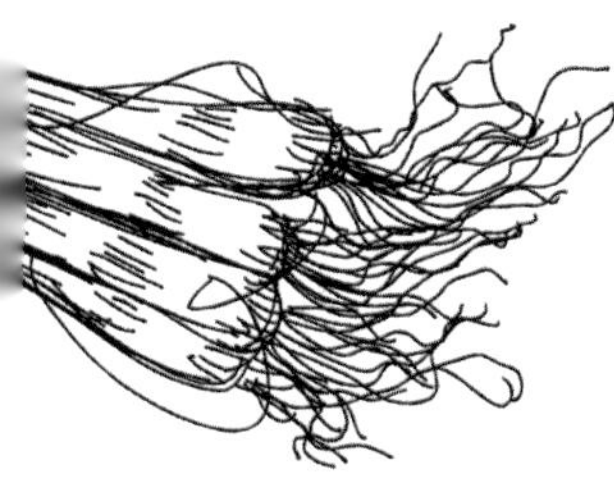

BALL PARK NACHOS

SERVES 4

Chain restaurants have made a mockery out of picadillo. Most fast-food nachos offer a ground beef topping that barely qualifies to be served to dogs, let alone served atop world-class nachos. To remedy this travesty try making this version of Ball Park Nachos instead.

Picadillo

½ cup raisins
1 pound ground beef
One 14½-ounce can diced tomatoes, with their juices
2 tablespoons chili powder
1½ teaspoons ground cinnamon
1 tablespoon ground cumin
Salt and black pepper
3 garlic cloves, diced
1 onion, diced
½ green bell pepper, seeded and diced
½ red bell pepper, seeded and diced
Juice of 1 lime

Nachos

7 ounces corn tortilla chips, approximately half of a store-bought bag, or, if prepared fresh, use 15 corn tortillas, each cut into 6 triangles
Picadillo (recipe above)
Béchamel Cheese Sauce (page 35), made with cheddar, warmed
¼ cup jarred pickled jalapeño peppers (optional)
½ cup sour cream
Simple Pico de Gallo (page 7)

To make the picadillo

1. Soak the raisins in water for 20 minutes to plump. Drain the liquid from the raisins before using.
2. Meanwhile, in a large skillet, cook the beef over medium heat until browned, making sure to break up any lumps. Drain the excess grease from the ground beef.
3. Stir in the diced tomatoes with their juices and the chili powder, cinnamon, and cumin. Season with salt and pepper to taste.
4. Cook the beef-tomato mixture for 8 to 10 minutes over medium-low heat until the liquid has reduced by half.
5. Add the garlic, onion, and peppers. Cook until the vegetables are tender and all of the liquid has cooked off, about 15 minutes.
6. Stir in the drained raisins and lime juice.

To assemble the nachos

1. Layer the tortilla chips in a 9 x 13-inch roasting pan. Evenly distribute the picadillo mixture over the tortilla chips, then cover the chips with the cheese sauce.
2. Garnish with the pickled jalapeños, if using, and serve with sour cream and the pico de gallo.

CARNE ASADA NACHOS

GLUTEN-FREE

SERVES 4

Carne Asada Marinade

¼ cup olive oil
½ cup red wine vinegar
Juice of 2 limes
Juice of 1 orange
½ cup water
3 garlic cloves, minced
1 jalapeño pepper, seeded and minced
1 tablespoon ground cumin
¼ teaspoon ground cloves
1 teaspoon chili powder
1 tablespoon ground black pepper
1 tablespoon salt
½ cup fresh chopped cilantro
1 pound skirt steak or flank steak

(continued)

This recipe is perfect for those hot summer nights. With the use of crumbled cotija cheese, there's no need to turn on the oven. These can even be served at room temperature so they are the perfect nachos to bring to that Fourth of July cookout.

To marinate the meat

1. Combine all of the ingredients for the marinade in a bowl and whisk to combine.
2. Place the meat in a gallon-size freezer bag or a nonreactive (plastic or glass) storage container with a lid.
3. Pour the marinade on top of the meat, then close the bag or cover the container and marinate in the refrigerator for at least 4 hours, preferably overnight.

To prepare the Carne Asada

1. Place a large stovetop grill pan over medium heat or on the grill in a grill basket. Brush the pan with olive oil.
2. Add the sliced onions to the pan, cover, and cook 3 minutes on each side. The onions should be charred on the edges. If you are using a grill pan, cover the onions with aluminum foil. Remove the onions from the pan and set aside.
3. Remove the meat from the marinade, and on a grill or stovetop grill pan, grill the meat for 3 minutes on each side over medium heat; the meat should be on the rare side. Transfer the meat to a cutting board and let rest for 5 minutes.
4. Thinly slice the steak on the diagonal across the grain, then in half, and then into 1-inch, bite-size pieces.

Nachos

- 1 pound marinated carne asada (page 66)
- Olive oil
- 4 onions, sliced
- 7 ounces corn tortilla chips, approximately half of a store-bought bag, or, if prepared fresh, use 15 corn tortillas, each cut into 6 triangles
- 8 ounces cotija cheese, crumbled
- ½ cup Basic Crema (page 119)
- ¼ cup fresh chopped cilantro
- 3 radishes, thinly sliced into rounds, about ¼ inch thick
- Juice of 1 lime

To assemble the nachos

1. Layer the tortilla chips on a 9 x 13-inch roasting pan. Evenly distribute the carne and onions over the chips. Cover the chips with the crumbled cotija cheese.
2. Drizzle the crema over the nachos prior to serving and garnish with cilantro and sliced radishes. Squeeze the lime juice over the nachos and serve.

BLACK AND BLUE BURGER NACHOS

SERVES 4

Elevate the cheeseburger by using blue cheese, mushrooms, and caramelized onions and then turning them into nachos! And don't skimp on the bacon.

1 tablespoon olive oil
2 medium yellow onions, thinly sliced
1 tablespoon unsalted butter
Salt and black pepper
1 cup cremini mushrooms, sliced
8 ounces bacon (about 8 slices)
1 pound ground beef
1 cup Béchamel Cheese Sauce (page 35), made with blue cheese, warmed
7 ounces corn tortilla chips, approximately half of a store-bought bag, or, if prepared fresh, use 15 corn tortillas, each cut into 6 triangles

1. In a large skillet over medium heat, heat the olive oil until shimmering.
2. Add the sliced onions and cook until caramelized, about 20 minutes.
3. After the onions have started to lightly brown, stir in the butter along with a pinch of salt and pepper.
4. Reduce the heat to medium-low. Add the mushrooms and cook, stirring occasionally, until the mushrooms have released their liquid and it has evaporated, about 15 minutes more.
5. While the onions and mushrooms cook, in a separate skillet, fry the bacon over medium heat until crispy on one side, 6 to 8 minutes on each side.
6. Once fully cooked, transfer the bacon to paper towels to drain and cool before coarsely chopping it. Reserve the bacon fat in the skillet.
7. Add the ground beef to the bacon fat and cook until browned, then drain the remaining oil.
8. As the beef browns, prepare the cheese sauce. Keep it covered until all the components are ready to use.
9. Layer the tortilla chips on a 9 x 13-inch baking sheet. Evenly distribute the onions and mushrooms over the tortilla chips, followed by the bacon and ground beef. Cover the chips with the warm cheese sauce.

PORTUGUESE NACHO HASH

Contributed by Kevin Chun, Executive Chef at Macao

GLUTEN-FREE

SERVES 4

1 tablespoon extra-virgin olive oil
4 to 6 ounces fresh linguiça (a Portuguese smoke-cured pork sausage), casings removed
½ cup julienned Vidalia onions
½ cup julienned piquillo or red bell peppers
1 tablespoon chopped Holland or Fresno chiles
1 tablespoon garlic, chopped
2 tablespoons pitted Spanish black olives, chopped
1 teaspoon smoked Spanish paprika
Salt and black pepper
½ cup chicken stock
1 cup shredded cheese (use your favorite type, I prefer a mix of sharp cheddar and Jack cheeses)
7 ounces corn tortilla chips, approximately half of a store-bought bag, or, if prepared fresh, use 15 corn tortillas, each cut into 6 triangles
2 tablespoons diced fresh tomatoes, for garnish (optional)
1 teaspoon chopped flat-leaf parsley, for garnish (optional)

This recipe is for those who just can't get enough of the gooey cheesy center of loaded nachos, and want to try it with a Portuguese twist.

1. Cook the linguiça in a large skillet over medium-high heat, breaking up any clumps, for 7 to 8 minutes until slightly browned.
2. Once the linguiça is cooked, add the onions, peppers, chiles, garlic, olives, and smoked paprika. Season with salt and pepper to taste. Continue to sauté on high heat for about 1 minute.
3. Add the chicken stock. Since the pan will be extremely hot, the chicken stock will immediately start to evaporate. Once the stock has reduced by about half remove from the heat and immediately add the cheese.
4. Quickly add the chips to the pan and toss everything together, until the cheese is completely melted and each chip is coated. Be careful not to break the chips while doing this. Season with additional salt and pepper if needed.
5. Serve immediately, garnished with diced fresh tomatoes and parsley, if using.

LETTUCE: OFFICIAL NACHO SPOILER

One of the top nacho fails of all time is iceberg lettuce. I despise "wedge salads" and find half a head of iceberg lettuce on my plate to be a waste of my limited stomach space. I'm not talking about carefully placed cilantro leaves or even (gasp) parsley, nor do I take issue with mesclun greens, spinach, or romaine lettuce. The only significant greenage I want to see on my nachos is some guac action with a kick of jalapeños.

If your chips are fresh and crispy, the crunch of lettuce is redundant. So put down the head of iceberg, step away from the salad bar, and leave my 'chos alone or heads will roll. *—Rachel*

BUFFALO CHICKEN NACHOS

GLUTEN-FREE

SERVES 4

Blue Cheese Sauce

- 2 tablespoons finely chopped onion
- 1 garlic clove, minced
- ¼ cup finely chopped flat-leaf parsley leaves
- ½ cup sour cream
- 1 cup mayonnaise
- 1 tablespoon fresh lemon juice
- 1 tablespoon white vinegar
- ¼ cup crumbled blue cheese
- 1 teaspoon cayenne pepper
- Salt and black pepper

Nachos

- 2 tablespoons melted unsalted butter
- ½ cup Frank's RedHot sauce
- 1 poached chicken breast, shredded (see box)
- Blue Cheese Sauce (recipe above)

(continued)

Buffalo wings are a point of pride all over western New York. To make matters more delicious, we added some blue cheese sauce and tortilla chips! If the heat is too much for you to take, add 2 tablespoons of ketchup to the hot sauce mixture before tossing it together with the chicken. Serve these bad boys during Monday Night Football and root for the Buffalo Bills as they take on the AFC East.

The blue cheese sauce in this recipe hails from the Anchor Bar in Buffalo, New York, home to the original Buffalo wing. This recipe will make more sauce than you'll need for the nachos, so, if you want, save some for a side of hot wings, too. —*Rachel*

7 ounces corn tortilla chips, approximately half of a store-bought bag, or, if prepared fresh, use 15 corn tortillas, each cut into 6 triangles
1 celery stalk, thinly sliced
2 scallions, white and green parts separated, chopped
4 ounces shredded cheddar cheese (about 1 cup)
¼ cup blue cheese crumbles
¼ cup coarsely chopped fresh cilantro

To make Blue Cheese Sauce

1. Mix together all of the ingredients for the sauce and refrigerate for at least 2 hours.
2. Bring the Blue Cheese Sauce to room temperature just before using it in the nachos recipe.

To assemble nachos

1. Preheat the oven to 350°F.
2. Toss the melted butter, hot sauce, and chicken with ¼ cup of the blue cheese sauce.
3. Layer the tortilla chips in a 9 x 13-inch roasting pan. Evenly distribute the chicken mixture, celery slices, and chopped white scallions over the chips. Cover the chips with the shredded cheddar cheese.
4. Bake the nachos for 10 to 15 minutes until the cheese has melted.
5. Top the nachos with ½ cup of the Blue Cheese Sauce and the chopped green scallion tops. Sprinkle the blue cheese crumbles and the chopped cilantro on top just before serving.

HOW TO POACH CHICKEN BREASTS

Poaching chicken is the easiest and most consistent way to prepare chicken breasts for nachos. This recipe works for one chicken breast or ten. Just make sure you find an appropriate-size pan to fit the chicken.

1. Put the chicken breasts in a saucepan or large pot, and add water to cover.
2. Over high heat, bring the water to a boil, then reduce the heat to a simmer.
3. Cover the pot and simmer the chicken for 10 minutes.
4. Remove the pan from the heat and leave the chicken in the pot to finish cooking in the hot water for 10 to 15 minutes more.

BBQ CHICKEN NACHOS

GLUTEN-FREE

SERVES 4

Lick your fingers and get a little saucy with these nachos. It's a messy one, so grab a napkin, but don't you dare reach for that fork—use your fingers, and dig in.

1 cup favorite barbecue sauce, divided
1 pound poached chicken breast, shredded (see How to Poach Chicken Breasts, page 73)
1 small yellow onion, diced
1 jalapeño pepper, seeded and diced
7 ounces corn tortilla chips, approximately half of a store-bought bag, or, if prepared fresh, use 15 corn tortillas, each cut into 6 triangles
4 ounces cheddar cheese, shredded (about 1 cup)
4 ounces Monterey Jack cheese, shredded (about 1 cup)
½ avocado, pitted and sliced
½ bunch fresh cilantro, chopped
½ cup sour cream

1. Preheat the oven to 350°F.
2. In a small saucepan, warm ¾ cup of the barbecue sauce. Reserve the remaining ¼ cup and set aside.
3. Toss the cooked, shredded chicken with the warmed ¾ cup of the barbecue sauce until completely covered. Stir in the diced onion and jalapeño pepper and cook over medium heat for about 5 minutes, then set aside.
4. Layer the tortilla chips in a 9 x 13-inch roasting pan. Evenly distribute the chicken mixture over the chips. Cover the chips with the cheeses.
5. Bake in the oven for 15 minutes, or until the cheeses have melted.
6. Remove from the oven and drizzle the remaining ¼ cup of barbecue sauce over the chips. Garnish with the avocado slices and cilantro and serve with a side of sour cream.

JERK CHICKEN NACHOS

GLUTEN-FREE

SERVES 4

Jerk Chicken Marinade

2 scotch bonnet peppers, seeded and chopped
4 green scallion tops, chopped
1 small onion, chopped
4 large garlic cloves, chopped
2 tablespoons chopped fresh thyme leaves
2 teaspoons ground allspice
2 teaspoons ground cinnamon
2 teaspoons ground nutmeg
2 teaspoons ground ginger
2 teaspoons black pepper
2 tablespoons salt
Juice of 3 limes
1 cup white vinegar
½ cup olive oil
½ cup water

(continued)

Scotch bonnet peppers are what give these nachos their kick and make them such jerks! Be careful when cutting hot peppers such as scotch bonnets as the spiciness can irritate your skin.

To marinate the chicken

1. In a bowl, whisk all of the ingredients for the marinade to combine.
2. Place the chicken in a gallon-size freezer bag or a nonreactive (plastic or glass) storage container with a lid.
3. Pour the marinade on top of the chicken, then close the bag or cover the container, and let marinate in the refrigerator for at least 4 hours, preferably overnight.

To prepare the chicken and mango

1. Preheat the oven to 350°F.
2. Remove the chicken from the jerk marinade and grill over medium heat. The most authentic way to prepare jerk chicken is over charcoal. However, a grill pan or outdoor grill works for this recipe as well.
3. Grill each side for approximately 15 minutes or until the internal temperature registers 165°F on an instant-read thermometer.
4. Allow the chicken to cool for 5 minutes, then shred it with a fork.
5. While the chicken is grilling, in a food processor or using an immersion blender, coarsely puree the mango, lime juice, and cayenne into a slaw-like texture.

To assemble the nachos

1. Layer the tortilla chips in a 9 x 13-inch roasting pan. Evenly distribute the chicken and mango mixture over the chips. Cover the chips with the shredded cheese.
2. Bake the nachos for 15 minutes, or until the cheese has melted.
3. Pair with the Simple Pico de Gallo and Simple Guacamole.

Nachos

1 pound jerk-marinated chicken breast (page 76)

1 mango, pitted, peeled, and chopped

Juice of 1 lime

¼ teaspoon cayenne pepper

7 ounces corn tortilla chips, approximately half of a store-bought bag, or, if prepared fresh, use 15 corn tortillas, each cut into 6 triangles

8 ounces Monterey Jack cheese, shredded (about 2 cups)

Simple Pico de Gallo (page 7)

Simple Guacamole (page 18)

CHICKEN CHORIZO NACHOS

GLUTEN-FREE

SERVES 4

2 chicken chorizo sausage links (about ½ pound), casings removed
7 ounces corn tortilla chips, about half of a store-bought bag, or, if prepared fresh, use 15 corn tortillas, each cut into 6 triangles
5 scallions, white and green parts separated, chopped
8 ounces cheddar cheese, shredded (about 2 cups)
¼ cup Easy Pickled Red Cabbage (page 122)
¼ cup Avocado-Horseradish Crema (page 120)
½ lime

Chicken chorizo typically has a milder flavor and pairs well with the scallions and pickled cabbage in this recipe. We used chicken chorizo from Brooklyn Cured, which was founded by Scott Bridi. You can find his chorizo and other charcuterie at www.brooklyncured.com.

1. Preheat the oven to 350°F.
2. Cook the chorizo in a large skillet over medium heat, breaking up any clumps, for 7 to 8 minutes until slightly browned. Drain off excess fat and allow the chorizo to cool until easy to handle.
3. Layer the tortilla chips in a 9 x 13-inch roasting pan. Evenly distribute the chorizo and the chopped white parts of the scallions over the chips. Cover the chips with the shredded cheese.
4. Bake the nachos for 10 to 15 minutes until the cheese has melted.
5. Evenly distribute the pickled cabbage over the finished nachos. Drizzle the crema over the nachos and garnish with the remaining scallion greens. Squeeze the juice of the lime over the nachos and serve.

FRIED CHICKEN NACHOS

SERVES 4

- 2 small boneless, skinless chicken breasts (about 1 pound)
- 1½ cups buttermilk
- 3 to 4 cups all-purpose flour
- Vegetable oil, for frying
- 7 ounces corn tortilla chips, about half of a store-bought bag, or, if prepared fresh, use 15 corn tortillas, each cut into 6 triangles
- One 15-ounce can refried beans
- 8 ounces cheddar cheese, shredded (about 2 cups)
- ½ cup Jalapeño Buttermilk Ranch Dressing (page 121)
- Prepared coleslaw (optional)

Fried chicken makes everything better. It's no different for nachos. For vegetarians, substitute the chicken breast with two fried and diced avocados.

To marinate the chicken

1. Cut the chicken breasts into bite-size pieces, about 1 inch long and ½ inch wide.
2. Marinate the chicken pieces in the buttermilk in the refrigerator for at least 4 hours, or preferably overnight.

To prepare the chicken

1. Preheat the oven to 350°F. Once marinated, dredge the chicken in flour and fry the chicken in a deep fryer in vegetable oil heated to 350°F until golden brown. Allow the chicken to cool. When the chicken is cool enough to handle, assemble the nachos.

To assemble the nachos

1. Layer the tortilla chips in a 9 x 13-inch roasting pan. Evenly distribute the refried beans and fried chicken over the chips. Cover the chips with the shredded cheese.
2. Bake in the oven for 15 minutes until the cheese is melted.
3. Drizzle the ranch dressing over the nachos and garnish with coleslaw, if desired.

NACHOS WITH LAMB AND BLACK BEAN CHILI

Contributed by Melissa Clark, food columnist at *The New York Times*

GLUTEN-FREE

SERVES 12 OR MORE

2 tablespoons olive oil
1 pound ground lamb
¾ teaspoon kosher salt, plus more, as needed
½ teaspoon ground black pepper, plus more, as needed
1 onion, finely chopped
2 poblano peppers, seeded and diced (or 2 small green bell peppers)
1 small bunch fresh cilantro, cleaned
4 garlic cloves, finely chopped
2 small jalapeño peppers, seeded, if desired, and finely chopped
2 tablespoons chili powder, plus more as needed
1 teaspoon ground coriander
1 teaspoon ground cumin
1½ tablespoons tomato paste
4 cups water
3½ cups cooked black beans (homemade or canned)
7 ounces corn tortilla chips, approximately half of a store-bought bag, or, if prepared fresh, use 15 corn tortillas, each cut into 6 triangles
8 ounces cheddar cheese, shredded (about 2 cups), preferably goat's milk cheddar, for serving
Lime wedges, for serving

Everyone has had nachos with ground beef, but how about ground lamb? Courtesy of *New York Times* food columnist and cookbook author Melissa Clark, these nachos are perfect for a casual dinner party.

1. Heat the oil in the bottom of a soup pot over medium-high heat. Add the lamb and cook, breaking it up with a fork, until well browned, about 5 minutes. Season with ½ teaspoon each of salt and pepper. Transfer the meat to a paper towel–lined plate.
2. Add the onion and poblano peppers to the pot. Cook until the vegetables are softened, 5 to 7 minutes.
3. Finely chop 2 tablespoons of the cilantro stems and add to the pot. Stir in the garlic and jalapeños and cook for 2 minutes.
4. Add the chili powder, coriander, and cumin and cook for 1 minute.
5. Stir in the tomato paste and cook until it begins to turn golden brown.
6. Return the lamb to the pot.
7. Stir in the water, beans, and the remaining ¼ teaspoon salt. Simmer over medium-low heat for 45 minutes; add more water if the chili becomes too thick. Taste and adjust the seasonings, if necessary.
8. Preheat the broiler to 500°F.
9. Arrange the tortilla chips on a baking sheet. Spoon the chili over the top and sprinkle with the cheese.
10. Broil for 1 to 2 minutes, until the cheese melts and bubbles.
11. Garnish with chopped cilantro leaves and serve with lime wedges.

CHORIZO AND MANCHEGO NACHOS

GLUTEN-FREE

SERVES 4

My favorite discovery since Nachos NY began is my love of chorizo. It tastes excellent with everything, especially here with the Manchego. —*Lee*

1 tablespoon vegetable oil
2 garlic cloves, minced
½ onion, diced
½ pound fresh chorizo, casings removed
7 ounces corn tortilla chips, approximately half of a store-bought bag, or, if prepared fresh, use 15 corn tortillas, each cut into 6 triangles
½ pound Manchego cheese, shredded
1 Pickled Serrano Pepper (page 122), sliced
Simple Guacamole (page 18)

1. In a skillet over medium heat, heat the vegetable oil, then add the diced garlic cloves and the onion.
2. When the garlic and onion become translucent, add the chorizo, breaking it up as it browns.
3. Preheat the broiler to 500°F.
4. Layer the tortilla chips in a 9 x 13-inch roasting pan. Evenly distribute the chorizo over the chips, followed by the shredded cheese. Add the sliced serrano pepper on top.
5. Place the chips under the broiler and broil for 8 minutes.
6. Serve with the Simple Guacamole.

HAWAIIAN NACHOS

GLUTEN-FREE

SERVES 4

2 tablespoons vegetable oil
1 ham steak (about 1 pound)
7 ounces corn tortilla chips, approximately half of a store-bought bag, or, if prepared fresh, use 15 corn tortillas, each cut into 6 triangles
Roasted Pineapple Salsa (page 14)
8 ounces cheddar cheese, shredded (about 2 cups)
½ cup plain Greek yogurt

I never could get behind Hawaiian pizza. However, when I was camping as a kid, we would make grilled cheese sandwiches with American cheese, deli ham, pineapple rings, and tomato sauce and they were delicious. Replace the American cheese with cheddar, and you have Nachos NY's little piece of tropical paradise. —*Rachel*

1. Preheat the oven to 350°F.
2. In a large skillet over medium-high heat, heat the vegetable oil, then add the ham steak and cook for about 4 minutes on each side.
3. Remove the ham from the pan and chop it into ½-inch cubes.
4. Layer the tortilla chips in a 9 x 13-inch roasting pan or on a baking sheet. Evenly distribute the cubed ham and the Roasted Pineapple Salsa over the chips. Cover the chips with the shredded cheese.
5. Bake the nachos for 10 to 15 minutes until the cheese has melted.
6. Add the Greek yogurt and serve.

CARNITAS NACHOS

Contributed by Richard Sloven, Gorilla Guac

GLUTEN-FREE

SERVES 8 TO 10

Carnitas

4 to 5 pounds pork butt, cut into 4 pieces
2 large yellow onions, quartered
6 whole garlic cloves
1 navel orange, quartered
One 12-ounce can tomato sauce
¼ cup salt
1 tablespoon ground black pepper
1 tablespoon ground cumin

Nachos

7 ounces corn tortilla chips, approximately half of a store-bought bag, or, if prepared fresh, use 15 corn tortillas, each cut into 6 triangles
Refried Beans (page 121)
3 cups shredded cheddar and Monterey Jack cheeses (about 12 ounces)
Carnitas (recipe above)
Sour cream, for serving
Simple Guacamole (page 18)
Simple Pico de Gallo (page 7)

Richard Sloven, also known as "Gorilla Guac," is best known for his made-to-order guacamole prepared on the streets of San Francisco and Brooklyn. Richard brings his talents indoors for this recipe. Allow yourself ample time to prepare this dish as the pork takes a while to braise.

To prepare the carnitas

1. Combine all of the ingredients for the carnitas in a large pot, and add enough water to completely immerse the pork.
2. Bring to a boil, reduce to the lowest heat, and simmer for 4 hours.
3. After 4 hours it should be effortless to stick a fork straight through the pork. If the meat is not tender enough, continue to simmer for another hour.
4. Remove the pork from the pot, cool, and place it in the fridge for an hour. (If you are preparing this the night before, cover the pork and leave overnight in the fridge.)
5. Preheat the oven to 450°F.
6. With two forks, pull the pieces of meat apart into small, shredded chunks.
7. Place all the chunks in a roasting pan, along with any drippings, and put in the oven for about 10 minutes.
8. Remove the roasting pan from the oven and stir the meat so it can brown on both sides. Return to the oven for another 5 to 10 minutes. Remove from the oven when the meat is brown and crisp.

To assemble the nachos

1. Preheat the oven to 350°F.
2. Cover an entire baking sheet with chips. Using a spoon, dollop the Refried Beans liberally on the chips. Cover the chips with a layer

of the shredded cheeses. Spread the carnitas out over the layer of cheese.

3. Place the baking sheet in the oven on the lowest rack and bake for about 5 minutes, or until the cheese is completely melted.
4. Remove from the oven and add several dollops of sour cream, guacamole, and pico de gallo.

PORK GINGER NACHOS

GLUTEN-FREE

SERVES 4

My favorite food that Nozomi, my Japanese fiancée/wife (depending on when you're reading this), makes is Pork Ginger. She gets the assist on this ginger-centric recipe. —*Lee*

1 tablespoon soy sauce
1 tablespoon mirin
1 tablespoon sake
½ pound pork cutlet
3 tablespoons fresh ginger, peeled and diced
1 tablespoon vegetable oil
¼ cup daikon
3 leaves shiso
½ small red onion
1 finger pepper
½ cup Basic Crema (page 119)
7 ounces tortilla chips, approximately half of a store-bought bag, or if prepared fresh, use 15 corn tortillas, each cut into 6 triangles
½ cup queso fresco, crumbled
Dried seaweed (optional)

1. In a small bowl, mix together the soy sauce, mirin, and sake. Pour the mixture into a large bowl with the pork cutlet and 2 tablespoons of the ginger and mix together with your hands.
2. In a skillet over medium heat, heat the oil. Add the pork with the ginger and sauce and cook until brown, 10 to 15 minutes.
3. On a cutting board, dice the pork into small pieces.
4. In a food processor fitted with the metal blade, finely dice the daikon, shiso, red onion, and finger pepper.
5. Add the remaining 1 tablespoon ginger to the Basic Crema recipe to make a ginger crema.
6. Preheat the oven to 350°F.
7. Lay out the chips on a baking sheet. Drizzle crema over the chips, followed by the pork ginger and then the daikon-onion mix. Sprinkle the queso fresco on top. Bake in oven for 8 minutes. Garnish with seaweed on top, if using.

AUTUMNAL NACHOS

VEGETARIAN • GLUTEN-FREE

SERVES 4

½ butternut squash
2 tablespoons maple syrup
½ teaspoon cayenne pepper
½ teaspoon ground cumin
1 tablespoon unsalted butter
1 large red onion, thinly sliced
1 teaspoon sugar
¼ cup balsamic vinegar
Salt and black pepper
7 ounces corn tortilla chips, approximately half of a store-bought bag, or, if prepared fresh, use 15 corn tortillas, each cut into 6 triangles
6 ounces shredded Gruyère cheese (about 1½ cups)
¼ cup sour cream

For optimal nacho flavors, choose seasonal ingredients. In the fall, after you have finished raking the leaves, reward yourself with these autumnal nachos while enjoying a good pumpkin ale.

1. Preheat the oven to 425°F.
2. Peel the butternut squash and then cut it in half lengthwise. Remove the seeds and fibers from the center. Thinly slice the squash and then cut it in half again lengthwise.
3. In a medium bowl, toss the squash with the maple syrup, cayenne, and cumin.
4. Place the squash on a parchment paper- or aluminum foil-lined baking sheet. Roast the squash for 20 minutes, or until tender.
5. While the squash is roasting, melt the butter in a skillet. Add the onion and cook over moderate heat until a deep brown color, 10 to 15 minutes. Be careful not to burn the onion.
6. Stir in the sugar and balsamic vinegar and season with a bit of salt and pepper. Cook the onion for an additional 10 to 15 minutes, stirring occasionally.
7. Reduce the oven temperature to 350°F.
8. Layer the tortilla chips on a 9 x 13-inch baking sheet. Evenly distribute the squash and onion over the chips. Cover the chips with the shredded cheese.
9. Bake the nachos for 10 to 15 minutes until the cheese has melted.
10. Serve the nachos with sour cream on the side.

ROASTED BEET, APPLE, AND GOAT CHEESE NACHOS

VEGETARIAN

SERVES 4

2 red beets, diced
1 yellow onion, diced
2 tablespoons olive oil
Salt and black pepper
7 ounces corn tortilla chips, about half of a store-bought bag, or, if prepared fresh, use 15 corn tortillas, each cut into 6 triangles
½ green apple, thinly sliced
Béchamel Cheese Sauce (page 35), made with goat cheese
Juice of 1 lime

Beets make a wonderful addition to nachos. The acidity of the green apples helps balance out the earthiness of the beets and complements the béchamel goat cheese sauce. If you simply cannot get enough beet action, enjoy these with The Joker guacamole (page 22).

1. Preheat the oven to 400°F.
2. Toss the beets and onion with olive oil, and season with salt and pepper.
3. Roast the beets and onion on a parchment paper- or aluminum foil-lined pan for 35 to 40 minutes, turning once or twice until the beets are easily pierced with a fork.
4. Remove the pan from the oven and drain the excess oil.
5. Layer the tortilla chips in a 9 x 13-inch roasting pan. Evenly distribute the beets and onion and the sliced green apple over the chips. Cover the chips with the goat cheese sauce.
6. Pour the lime juice over the nachos just before serving as the final touch.

IRISH NACHOS

SERVES 6 TO 8

One 20- to 22-ounce bag frozen waffle fries
½ pound of bacon (about 8 slices), coarsely chopped
2 scallions, whites and greens separated, chopped
4 ounces Monterey Jack cheese, shredded (about 1 cup)
4 ounces cheddar cheese, shredded (about 1 cup)
2 tablespoons chopped fresh cilantro, for garnish
½ cup sour cream, for garnish

Yes, Irish Nachos are not really nachos, per se, they have a potato base instead of the conventional corn tortilla chips. But who can say no to cheese, bacon, onions, and sour cream? This waffle-fries version is a spin on a dish served at a college bar in Poughkeepsie, New York. Many nights a hangover has been averted, in part by the starchy goodness of Irish Nachos. Dig in and don't hate us for calling these bad boys nachos.

1. Prepare the frozen waffle fries according to the package directions.
2. Meanwhile, fry the bacon in a skillet over medium heat until crispy, 6 to 8 minutes on each side. Transfer the bacon to paper towels to drain and cool before coarsely chopping.
3. Preheat the broiler to 500°F.
4. Arrange the waffle fries on a baking sheet. Top the waffle fries with the chopped white parts of the scallions, then the chopped bacon, followed by the shredded Monterey Jack and cheddar cheeses.
5. Place the waffle fries under the broiler for 5 minutes.
6. Just before serving, garnish the nachos with the chopped green scallion tops, the cilantro, and the sour cream.

IRISH NACHOS TAKE 2

GLUTEN-FREE

SERVES 4

5 slices bacon
3 potatoes, sliced ½ inch thick
12 deli sliced pieces smoked Gouda cheese (about ½ pound)
2 scallions, white and green parts separated, chopped
½ cup sour cream, for garnish

Proceed with caution when eating these nachos, or at least wear pants with an elastic waistband! These nachos may not be your arteries' best friends, so make sure you enjoy them in moderation and break out the silverware to share with friends. Instead of waffle fries, here we use thick-sliced potatoes to serve as the "chips."

1. Preheat the oven to 350°F.
2. In a skillet, fry the bacon over medium heat until crispy, 6 to 8 minutes on each side.
3. Transfer the bacon to paper towels to drain and cool. Reserve the fat in the skillet.
4. Fry the sliced potatoes in the reserved bacon fat until brown, about 6 minutes on each side.
5. Drain any excess fat from the skillet.
6. Evenly layer the potato slices in the skillet. Top the potatoes with ½ of the smoked Gouda, followed by the chopped white parts of the scallions and then the bacon strips. Cover the bacon with the remaining Gouda cheese.
7. Bake the nachos for 10 to 15 minutes until cheese has melted.
8. Remove from the oven and garnish with the chopped green tops of the scallions and the sour cream.

DESSERT NACHOS

Nachos for dessert, what could be sweeter? When I am not eating nachos at a bar or making batches of cheese sauce to get me through the week, I bake cupcakes for a living. My days are filled with chocolate batter, buttercream, and salted caramel. Working for Robicelli's in Brooklyn, New York, my bosses' philosophy on cupcakes is to create small, portable, and accessible desserts that incorporate a wide variety of flavors and experiences. Yes, we do Chicken 'n' Waffles cupcakes, but we also make a fig cake with goat cheese buttercream, crisped prosciutto, and fig balsamic *gastrique.* We make classy foods available to the common people.

That's the sort of view I took when creating recipes like the Poached Pear and Gorgonzola Nachos recipe. Poached pears are delicious on their own and are super easy to make. The same goes for ganache. It's fancy sounding, right? But basically, ganache is heavy cream and chocolate. Hell, you can make it in a microwave and put it on crappy ice cream and you'll look like an ice cream savior. Mascarpone cheese is phenomenal right out of the container, but if you'd like, dollop a little on some leftover poached pear from the nachos recipe and you have another sweet little treat. Elevate your desserts and allow yourself to have nachos for every meal while learning a few tricks of the trade.

—Rachel

CHOCO-NACHO

VEGETARIAN • GLUTEN-FREE

SERVES 4

16 perfect chips; if prepared fresh, use 4 corn tortillas, each cut into 4 triangles

Chocolate Cayenne Ganache

3½ ounces semisweet chocolate, chopped
½ cup heavy cream
1½ teaspoons cayenne pepper

Goat's Milk Caramel (Cajeta)

¼ teaspoon baking soda
1 tablespoon water
2 cups goat's milk
½ cup sugar
1 teaspoon vanilla extract

These tortilla chips are covered in chocolate ganache. Chocolate ganache sounds fancy and difficult, but all it takes is heavy cream and semisweet chocolate. For fun, change up the recipe by adding cinnamon, orange liqueur, or instant coffee. You can even drizzle the sauces over ice cream, or stir them into your morning coffee. These Choco-Nachos pair perfectly with a side of vanilla-bean ice cream.

To make the ganache

MICROWAVE METHOD

1. In a microwave safe bowl, combine the chopped chocolate and heavy cream.
2. Microwave until the chocolate starts to melt, about 1 minute.
3. Stir and continue to microwave at 15-second intervals until smooth. Be careful not to burn the ganache. If it burns, there's no way to save it.
4. When the ganache is melted and smooth, add the cayenne.

STOVETOP METHOD

1. Fill a medium saucepan halfway with water and bring to a simmer over low heat.
2. Add the chopped chocolate and cream to a heatproof glass bowl. Place over the saucepan of simmering water; the bottom of the bowl should not touch the water. Stir the ganache mixture until melted.
3. Once it has melted, remove the bowl from the saucepan, add the cayenne, and stir the ganache until smooth. The ganache can be stored in the refrigerator for up to 2 weeks and reheated when needed.

(continued)

To make the caramel

1. In a small bowl, dissolve the baking soda with 1 tablespoon of water and set aside.
2. In a medium saucepan over medium-high heat combine the goat's milk, sugar, and vanilla. Stir regularly until the milk comes to a simmer and the sugar has dissolved.
3. Remove the saucepan from the heat and stir in the baking soda and water mixture carefully, continuing to stir to keep the mixture from bubbling over.
4. Reduce the heat to medium and continue to cook the caramel, stirring regularly, until the mixture turns pale golden, about 20 minutes.

To assemble the Choco-Nachos

1. Dip each tortilla chip in melted ganache halfway. Repeat this step for all 16 chips, placing them on a wire cooling rack to allow the ganache to set.
2. Once the ganache has set, drizzle the cajeta over each chip.

BOILING IT DOWN: REDUCTIONS

In the following recipes, you'll learn how to make a reduction. Think of a reduction as a concentrate. Not quite orange juice concentrate, but close. By cooking down a liquid such as wine or balsamic vinegar, excess water is evaporated, creating a syrup-like consistency. All the flavor from the initial bottle of wine or balsamic vinegar is now packed into just a few tablespoons. Why do this? Well, imagine if you poured an entire bottle of wine over a scoop of ice cream. Nasty. But reduce it down, and you retain and intensify all of the flavor without your ice cream swimming in booze.

POACHED PEAR AND GORGONZOLA NACHOS

VEGETARIAN • GLUTEN-FREE

SERVES 4

1½ cups red wine, preferably something fruity like a Merlot
1 ripe but firm pear
16 perfect chips; if prepared fresh, use 4 corn tortillas, each cut into 4 triangles
2 ounces Gorgonzola cheese, crumbled, preferably Gorgonzola Dolce (about ⅓ cup)
2 tablespoons honey

Nachos can be used as a gateway to preparing other foods. Yes, we want you to love chips, cheese, and guacamole, but you should also learn a new skill or two, like how to poach a pear or roast a red pepper. In addition to using pears as a component in nachos, poached pears are great on their own as a simple dessert with fresh vanilla-flavored whipped cream.

1. In a saucepan, bring the red wine to a boil. Once the wine is boiling, reduce the heat to a simmer, and add the pear.
2. Simmer the pear for 10 minutes, then turn it, and simmer for 10 minutes more or until it is tender and easily pierced with the tip of a sharp knife.
3. Remove the pear from the wine and set aside and let cool.
4. While the pear is cooling, reduce the wine by half, or until it has a syrup-like consistency, 7 to 8 minutes.
5. Once cooled, slice the pear in half, then into thin slivers, for a total of 16 slices. Be careful not to include any of the core or seeds!
6. Preheat the broiler to 500°F.
7. Arrange the chips on a serving dish. Evenly distribute the pears over the chips and top with the crumbled Gorgonzola.
8. Broil the nachos for 5 minutes. Gorgonzola burns quickly, so keep an eye on it!
9. Remove from the oven, drizzle the wine reduction and honey over the nachos, and serve.

STRAWBERRY, BASIL, AND MASCARPONE DESSERT NACHOS

VEGETARIAN • GLUTEN-FREE

SERVES 4

½ cup strawberries, hulled and diced (about 6 large berries)
1 tablespoon chiffonade of fresh basil
1 tablespoon sugar, plus 1 teaspoon for the balsamic reduction
½ cup balsamic vinegar
1 cup mascarpone cheese
16 blue corn tortilla chips

Here's a way to your lover's heart: mascarpone. Creamy and subtly sweet, you can pair mascarpone with strawberries and basil as in this recipe or the red wine poached pear (page 99) and enjoy as a snack, or just spread some on a chocolate chip cookie.

1. Combine the diced strawberries, basil, and 1 tablespoon of the sugar in a small bowl to create a strawberry-basil salsa.
2. Let it macerate while you prepare the balsamic reduction.
3. In a sauté pan over medium heat, combine the vinegar with the remaining 1 teaspoon sugar. Reduce the balsamic vinegar by half, 3 to 4 minutes; be careful not to burn it. Allow the reduction to cool before using.
4. Spoon approximately 1 tablespoon of mascarpone cheese on each individual chip. A melon baller or small ice cream scoop works perfectly here.
5. Top the cheese with some strawberry-basil salsa.
6. Drizzle the reduction over each chip.

SWEET CORN ICE CREAM

VEGETARIAN • GLUTEN-FREE

SERVES 8

1½ cups corn kernels (about 3 ears fresh corn)
1 cup heavy cream
1½ cups whole milk
½ cup sugar
4 large egg yolks
¼ cup Candied Jalapeños (page 124)

When I was growing up, we had pay-and-take stands for fresh sweet corn near our house. Summer meant sweet corn for dinner almost every night. Still warm from the sun, nothing beats it. Serve this ice cream with unsalted, homemade corn tortilla chips instead of a sugar or waffle cone. —*Rachel*

1. Remove the kernels from the fresh ears of corn using a box grater.
2. In a medium saucepan over medium heat, combine the cream, milk, and corn and bring to a simmer.
3. While the cream mixture is coming to a simmer, in a medium bowl, whisk together the sugar and egg yolks until pale and thick.
4. When the cream mixture reaches a simmer, slowly add ½ cup into the egg mixture, whisking constantly to temper the eggs. Repeat, adding the remaining sugar and egg mixture.
5. Reduce the heat to low, whisk the warmed egg mixture back into the saucepan, and cook, until the mixture thickens, about 5 minutes, whisking constantly.
6. Pour the mixture into a medium bowl and chill for at least 2 hours and up to 1 day.
7. Freeze the chilled ice cream base in an ice cream maker according to manufacturer's instructions.
8. When the ice cream has almost finished spinning, add the Candied Jalapeños.
9. Serve the ice cream immediately with unsalted corn tortilla chips, or transfer to an airtight plastic container and freeze for later use.

AVOCADO ICE CREAM

VEGETARIAN • GLUTEN-FREE

SERVES 8

Avocados aren't just for guacamole. If desired, throw in ¼ cup of toasted dried coconut or even frozen pineapple while you are spinning the ice cream. This will add some texture and a burst of flavor.

3 medium-ripe avocados, halved lengthwise, pitted, and flesh scooped out
One 14-ounce can coconut milk
½ cup heavy cream
Juice of 3 limes (about 2 tablespoons)
¾ cup sugar

1. Using an immersion blender or a food processor, puree all of the ingredients until smooth.
2. Freeze the mixture in an ice cream maker according to manufacturer's instructions; it sets up really quickly and you don't want to overmix it, so only process it for 5 to 10 minutes. If you want a firmer texture, freeze the ice cream for at least 2 hours before serving.

TORTILLA CHIP TORTE

Contributed by Jessie Oleson from *CakeSpy*

VEGETARIAN

SERVES 8

Torte

16 tablespoons (2 sticks) unsalted butter
2 tablespoons granulated sugar
1 tablespoon cocoa powder (Dutch process is fine)
2 teaspoons ground cinnamon
Pinch of salt
Four 10-inch flour tortillas

Filling and Topping

2 cups dark chocolate morsels or chunks (about 12 ounces)
4 cups sour cream (don't even insult me by using low fat)
1 cup confectioners' sugar, sifted
Chocolate shavings and fresh strawberries, for garnish (optional)

For a sweet snack that really takes the cake, you can dress up your nachos as a fancy tortilla torte. It takes a little time to prepare, but with layers of buttery chocolate nachos, sandwiched with a rich chocolate cream filling, and capped off with a tangy sour cream frosting, it's "nacho" typical cake, and is certainly a dessert to remember.

1. Preheat the oven to 400°F.
2. In a medium saucepan, melt the butter. Mix in the granulated sugar, cocoa powder, cinnamon, and salt and stir until completely incorporated. Using a pastry brush, brush the mixture over the tortillas. Then slice each tortilla into 6 "chips" and bake for 6 to 10 minutes. (You want them crispy but not too brown.) Set aside to cool while you prepare the filling.
3. In a medium saucepan, melt the chocolate over low heat, stirring occasionally. Stir in 2 cups of the sour cream. Remove from the heat, and cool for about 10 minutes.
4. Place the tortilla chips on a plate in a circular pie shape, making sure the tortillas only overlap each other once, otherwise the torte will get too thick and heavy. Keep the cake around 8 inches in diameter; it just gets way too unwieldy if it is larger! Spoon about ⅓ cup of the torte filling mixture on top, working delicately, as the tortilla chips will want to spread all over.
5. Cover this layer with another row of tortilla chips, trying to keep it as flat as possible; you can even gently crush the tortilla chips down on the previous layer.
6. Cover this layer with another ⅓ cup of the filling mixture.
7. Repeat using the remaining tortilla chips and filling until you've used it all. This will look ugly, but I promise it will be OK. Put it in the fridge for 1 hour or so, so it can all adhere together and the chips can soften from the chocolate mixture.

8. Remove the torte from the fridge, and using a large, sharp serrated knife, trim the edges so that the torte forms a nice round. Toss the scraps, or snack on them.
9. In a medium mixing bowl, stir together the remaining 2 cups sour cream and the confectioners' sugar. Frost the torte with the mixture. Garnish with chocolate shavings and strawberries, if desired.

NACHOS PANNA COTTA

SERVES 4

Four ½-pint glass jars or ramekins
½ cup Jalapeño Jelly (page 124)
1 cup fresh corn kernels (about 2 ears shucked and scraped)
1½ cups whole milk
¼ cup sugar
One 2½ x 9-inch gelatin sheet or 1 teaspoon powdered gelatin
¼ cup sour cream

Panna cotta sounds superfancy, but in reality is nothing more than milk and/or cream mixed with some sugar and gelatin to set it all up. Gelatin sheets can be found in most specialty markets or online. They are much easier to use and keep better than powdered gelatin.

In order to see the beautiful green Jalapeño Jelly layer at the bottom, you can prepare the panna cotta in glass jars. If you don't have any, no sweat, your friends will be pleasantly surprised by the subtle heat at the bottom of a ramekin.

1. Spoon 2 tablespoons of Jalapeño Jelly into each glass jar.
2. Allow the jelly to set in the refrigerator while you prepare the panna cotta mixture.
3. In a small saucepan, heat the corn kernels, milk, and sugar and bring to a simmer. Remove from the heat.
4. In the meantime, soak the gelatin sheet, if using, in ice water for 5 minutes to bloom.
5. Squeeze out any excess water, if using the gelatin sheet, and add the sheet or the powdered gelatin to the hot milk mixture. Whisk to dissolve it, then allow the mixture to cool for 5 minutes.
6. Strain the milk mixture to remove the corn. Whisk in the sour cream.
7. Pour the panna cotta mixture on top of the set jelly and chill in the refrigerator for at least 2 hours, or until completely set.

DRINKS

Making nachos, guacamoles, and salsas really strikes up a thirst. So does eating them. In this section, find drinks to pair with your favorite food. While we love a spicy Peach-Habanero Margarita, perfecting our Horchata recipe was a lot more exciting. We found a way to please beer drinkers with Micheladas, wine fanatics with Pomegranate–Blood Orange Sangria, and liquor lovers with margarita recipes.

MARGARITA

SERVES 1

1 lime wedge
Salt (optional)
2 ounces tequila
1 ounce triple sec
2 ounces fresh lime juice (from about 2 limes)
1 cup ice cubes

This classic is always enjoyable when you're having a good day. But to be honest, it's even better on a bad day.

1. Run a lime wedge around the rim of a glass.
2. Dip the glass in salt, if using salt.
3. Mix together the tequila, triple sec, lime juice, and ice in a shaker.
4. Pour into the salt-rimmed glass.

PEACH-HABANERO MARGARITA

SERVES 4

2 habanero peppers
12 ounces tequila
Juice of 4 peaches (about 20 ounces fresh peach juice)
2 cups ice cubes
Juice of 1 lime
1 teaspoon agave syrup

Here's the summer party drink you've always been looking for. The sweet and spice will surprise you at every sip.

1. Cut the 2 peppers in half and put in a jar with the tequila for 1 day.
2. Juice the four peaches in a juicer.
3. In a large pitcher, combine the ice cubes, tequila, and peach juice. Stir rapidly.
4. Add the lime juice and agave syrup to taste. Serve in mason jars or margarita glasses with salted rims.

MICHELADA

SERVES 1

1 lime wedge
Salt for glass (optional)
½ cup ice cubes
Juice of 1 lime
12 ounces dark Mexican beer
Jalapeño hot sauce
Maggi

When it's too hot to make a margarita (and it does get that hot) you can pull this recipe out of your back pocket and bask in beverage pride. We used Maggi seasoning in this recipe. Maggi is similar to soy sauce and is used in Asian and Mexican recipes to add a deep, roasted flavor to your drink.

1. Moisten the rim of a glass with a lime slice and dip the glass into salt, if using.
2. In a glass combine the ice, lime juice, beer, hot sauce, and Maggi to taste.
3. Stir the drink rapidly and enjoy.

POMEGRANATE–BLOOD ORANGE SANGRIA

SERVES 8

One 750 ml bottle red wine, something fruity like a Cabernet Sauvignon or Merlot
3 blood oranges, sliced (2 for soaking, 1 for garnish)
½ cup brandy
1½ cups pomegranate juice
½ cup Simple Syrup (see Box)
Seeds of 1 pomegranate, for garnish

This sangria recipe represents how much I have grown up since college. In those days, I made sangria in a pot with a box of wine, a bottle of orange vodka, and enough Simple Syrup to hide the alcohol taste. Now I take the time to let all the ingredients meld together. You can almost feel the hangover kicking in, can't you? —*Rachel*

1. In a large pitcher, combine the wine and 2 of the sliced blood oranges.
2. Allow the wine to macerate for at least 4 to 6 hours in the refrigerator.
3. After the oranges have had a chance to soak in the wine, add the brandy, pomegranate juice, and Simple Syrup.
4. Stir all the ingredients together to make sure everything is evenly combined.
5. Serve the sangria in a glass over ice, garnished with pomegranate seeds and a sliced blood orange on the rim.

SIMPLE SYRUP

If you like sweet tea, or put sugar in your iced coffee, you should really keep Simple Syrup in your fridge at all times. Simple Syrup is just equal parts sugar and water. This recipe makes a little over 1 cup, but you can really make it in any amount.

1 cup granulated sugar
1 cup water

1. In a medium saucepan, combine the sugar and water.
2. Bring the mixture to a boil, stirring, until the sugar has dissolved.
3. Allow the syrup to cool before using in your favorite beverages.

HORCHATA

SERVES 4

This drink will improve your outlook on a hot summer's day. This is highly recommended if you get thirsty and it's too early for a margarita.

1 cup long-grain rice, rinsed and drained
1 cup blanched almonds
4 cinnamon sticks
1 quart water
¾ cup sugar
2 teaspoons vanilla extract
2 cups ice cubes
Ground cinnamon, to taste

1. Put the rice, almonds, and cinnamon sticks in a blender. Blend the mixture into a powder.
2. Add the water, sugar, and vanilla and blend for 90 seconds.
3. Chill the mixture overnight in the fridge.
4. Strain the liquid into glasses over ice cubes and serve, sprinkled with ground cinnamon to taste.

EXTRAS

Extras include all the little odds and ends that just don't fit neatly into the nacho order of the world, but we love them so much we want to use them in all sorts of ways. Feel free to experiment and add these to your nacho recipes freely.

BASIC CREMA

VEGETARIAN • GLUTEN-FREE

MAKES 2 CUPS CREMA

1 cup sour cream
1 cup heavy cream
1 teaspoon salt

Sour cream is an American addition to nachos whereas crema comes from South of the Border. Crema is a neccessary ingredient to a spicy nacho recipe. Remember, it's milk and dairy that neutralizes the heat of jalapeños and chiles.

1. In a small bowl, mix all of the ingredients together.
2. Cover with plastic wrap and allow to sit at room temperature for about 1 hour.
3. If not using right away, keep the crema covered and store in the refrigerator. Crema will keep for as long as the expiration dates stated on the sour cream and heavy cream. Before using it, bring the crema back to room temperature.

AVOCADO-HORSERADISH CREMA

VEGETARIAN • GLUTEN-FREE

MAKES 11/2 CUPS CREMA

1 avocado, halved lengthwise, pitted, and flesh scraped out
1 cup Basic Crema (page 119)
Juice of 1 lime
1 tablespoon chopped fresh cilantro leaves
½ teaspoon cayenne pepper
1½ teaspoons prepared horseradish

If you are not using this crema right away, cover with plastic wrap pressed directly on the surface to prevent it from browning. This recipe pairs well with the Chicken Chorizo Nachos (page 80).

1. Using an immersion blender, puree all of the ingredients in a bowl until smooth.
2. Allow the crema to come to room temperature before using.

THOUSAND ISLAND CREMA

VEGETARIAN • GLUTEN-FREE

MAKES 1/2 CUP CREMA

¼ cup mayonnaise
¼ cup buttermilk
1 tablespoon ketchup
1 teaspoon sugar
1 teaspoon sweet pickle relish
Salt and black pepper

Perfect on the Reuben or Rachel Nachos (page 45), you can use any extra on hamburgers as your own secret sauce.

1. Using an immersion blender or food processor, blend all of the ingredients together until smooth.
2. Bring the crema to room temperature before using.

JALAPEÑO BUTTERMILK RANCH DRESSING

VEGETARIAN • GLUTEN-FREE

MAKES 3/4 CUP DRESSING

¼ cup sour cream
¼ cup buttermilk
¼ cup mayonnaise
1 garlic clove
1 jalapeño pepper, stemmed and seeded
1 tablespoon chopped fresh cilantro
1 tablespoon fresh chives
Salt and black pepper

Pair this recipe with the Fried Chicken Nachos (page 79) or use it in place of your favorite ranch salad dressing for an added kick.

1. Using an immersion blender or food processor, blend all of the ingredients except for the salt and pepper together until smooth.
2. Season the dressing with salt and pepper to taste.

REFRIED BEANS

VEGAN • GLUTEN-FREE

MAKES 3 CUPS BEANS

One 15-ounce can pinto beans
1 tablespoon vegetable oil
1 small onion, diced
1 garlic clove, minced
1 chipotle chile in adobo sauce, diced (optional)

These are usually viewed as the gross pile of goop in a huge pot that no one wants to admit that they like, but in reality, they are easy to make and just as delicious as you secretly think.

1. Drain the water from the beans. Using a fork or wooden spoon, mash the beans in a bowl.
2. In a skillet, heat the vegetable oil, add the onion and garlic, and cook until they are soft and translucent.
3. Add the beans and simmer for 10 minutes.
4. If adventurous, add the chipotle pepper and stir to incorporate.

EASY PICKLED RED CABBAGE

VEGAN • GLUTEN-FREE

MAKES JUST OVER 1 PINT PICKLED CABBAGE

½ small head red cabbage, cored and shredded
1 cup sugar
1 cup white vinegar
1 teaspoon salt
1 cup water

Pickled red cabbage adds a pretty dash of purple to a plate of 'chos. Use this recipe for the Chicken Chorizo Nachos (page 78).

1. In a medium saucepan, stir together the cabbage, sugar, vinegar, salt, and water.
2. Bring to a boil, cover, and simmer over medium heat for 1 hour.

   Note: The pickled cabbage can be served immediately, or chilled and used within 1 week, or processed in boiling water to be made shelf stable.

PICKLED SERRANO PEPPERS

VEGAN • GLUTEN-FREE

MAKES 1 PINT PICKLED PEPPERS

4 serrano peppers
⅓ cup white vinegar
⅓ cup water
2 tablespoons sugar
2 tablespoons salt
2 tablespoons whole black peppercorns

Pickling can be overwhelming; however, you can make these pickled serrano peppers with just a little bit of patience, and then add them gleefully to any nacho platter.

1. Make small incisions in the peppers and place them in a sterilized pint mason jar.
2. In a small saucepan, bring the vinegar, water, sugar, salt, and peppercorns to a boil. Reduce the heat and simmer for 10 minutes.
3. Add the mixture to the jar of peppers and let it cool in the fridge.
4. Allow the serrano peppers to pickle for 1 week.

MANGO-CHIPOTLE SAUCE

VEGAN • GLUTEN-FREE

MAKES 1 PINT SAUCE

1 tablespoon vegetable oil
3 garlic cloves, diced
1 mango, pitted, peeled, and sliced
3½ ounces chipotle chiles in adobo sauce
Juice of 1 lime
2 ounces white vinegar (4 tablespoons)

This is the Trojan Horse of sauces: The sweetness of the mango unexpectedly leads to a barrage of chipotle spice.

1. In a small saucepan, heat the oil over medium heat and add the garlic cloves.
2. When the garlic is soft, add the mango and stir constantly for 8 minutes.
3. Remove the garlic-mango mixture from the saucepan and place in a blender. Liquefy the mixture in the blender along with the chipotle peppers, lime juice, and vinegar. Return the sauce to the pan and simmer for 10 minutes.
4. Put into a sterilized pint mason jar and cool in the fridge.

JALAPEÑO HOT SAUCE

VEGAN • GLUTEN-FREE

MAKES 2 CUPS SAUCE

1 tablespoon vegetable oil
½ cup diced onion
2 garlic cloves, minced
½ cup chopped carrots
¼ cup water
9 jalapeño peppers, stemmed and minced
½ cup distilled vinegar
¼ cup fresh lime juice (about 2 limes)

This easy hot sauce will come in handy when you need to spice up any nacho or michelada.

1. In a small saucepan, over medium-high heat, warm the oil. Add the onion and garlic and cook until soft and translucent, 1 to 2 minutes.
2. Add the carrots and water and bring the mixture to a boil. Reduce the heat and simmer until the carrots are soft.
3. Pour the mixture and the jalapeños into a blender, and puree together until smooth.
4. Return the puree to the saucepan, and add the vinegar and lime juice. Simmer for 5 minutes to combine the flavors.
5. Strain the sauce into sterilized bottles.
6. Cool the sauce in the fridge overnight.

JALAPEÑO JELLY

VEGAN • GLUTEN-FREE

MAKES 1 CUP JELLY

¼ pound jalapeño peppers (about 6 medium peppers, seeded), sliced
1¼ cups sugar
½ cup cider vinegar
3 drops green food coloring

I don't think you're ready for this jelly! Just kidding, you are way overdue. Jalapeño Jelly can be used for the Nachos Panna Cotta recipe (page 108), or as a spread on toast with a little cream cheese to help spice up your morning.

1. In a small saucepan, combine the peppers, sugar, and cider vinegar. Stir together to dissolve the sugar. Bring the mixture to a boil over high heat, and cook for 4 minutes. Watch it carefully so it does not boil over.
2. Remove from the heat and stir in the food coloring.
3. Ladle the jelly into a half-pint mason jar. The jelly will keep for 1 week in the fridge.

CANDIED JALAPEÑOS

VEGAN • GLUTEN-FREE

MAKES ABOUT 1 PINT CANDIED JALAPEÑOS

½ pound jalapeño peppers (about 8 medium)
⅓ cup cider vinegar
1 cup sugar
Juice of 1 lime
1 pint-sized mason jar, sterilized

Candied Jalapeños are spun into the Sweet Corn Ice Cream (page 102). Throw them in a margarita for a sweet, crunchy kick, or use them as a garnish on cakes.

1. Slice the jalapeño peppers into ¼-inch thick rounds.
2. Combine the vinegar, sugar, and lime juice in small saucepan. Bring to a boil over medium heat. Reduce the heat to low and simmer until the sugar is dissolved and the mixture is syrupy, about 5 minutes.
3. Add the jalapeños and bring the mixture back to a simmer. Cook for 3 to 4 minutes until the peppers are tender.
4. Using a slotted spoon, transfer the jalapeños to a sterilized pint mason jar.
5. Return the syrup to a boil and cook for 5 minutes more.
6. Ladle the hot syrup over the jalapeños in the jar and seal.

ACKNOWLEDGMENTS

From Lee

Nozomi—You were by my side every day listening to new ideas for recipes and essays. You've supported me whenever I was panicking about a deadline or an upcoming event.

Mom and Dad—Since a young age, I have loved nachos, and you introduced me to them. Thanks for the introduction.

Katy, Grandmom Phyllis, Grandmom Ruthie, and Grandpop Milton—You always asked about our next event and what new things were happening in Nacholand even though my life revolved around nachos.

For all of my friends who have been listening to me talk about nachos for the past six, ten, forever years, thanks for remaining interested all this time.

From Rachel

It goes without question that my mom and dad continue to inspire and motivate me to be a better and busier person every day.

Thank you to Aunt Bet, Stan, Uncle Billy, Genie, and Carl, who have supported me while my parents were off being awesome.

I credit my boos, Monique and Siobhan, for our beach days at the Rockaways, which kept me sane throughout this whole process, and I'm grateful to Yoji for coming into my life at the right moment.

And last, but never least in my mind, Matt and Allison Robicelli for "taking care of me" when I was laid off and didn't know what to do next. Apparently, it was make cupcakes, write a book, and never look back.

From both of us

This nacho book didn't seem like a possibility without the help of so many people:

Jason—Nearly two years ago was the first time we met, and you immediately saw that there was a nacho book to be written and we were the ones to do it.

Karen—Thanks for your skills behind the camera and being available and incredibly helpful throughout the whole process.

Sophia—Your able hands in the kitchen made our tasty foods as beautiful as any nacho ever was.

Perry—You've provided your illustrations for us before. We were so excited you were able to come in at the last minute this time.

To our awesome contributors—thanks for being a part of the nacho agenda.

For everyone who has helped us put on an event—Maraysa, Heather, Leah, Caroline, Dan, Jenna, and countless others—you guys helped us get off the ground with support and advice every step of the way. We'd be avocado-less without you.

INDEX

H

I

J

L

M

N

O

P

Q

R

S

T

V

W